SY 0044244 5

D0726670

MARY'S COLLEGE LIBRARY
BT12 6FE

LVED AT

920

MOO

55342

A

55342.

First published 1990 by
Poolbeg Press Ltd.
Knocksedan House,
Swords, Co Dublin, Ireland
Reprinted February, 1990

© Sheila Mooney 1990

ISBN 1 85371 076 8

All rights reserved. No part of this publication may be
reproduced or transmitted in any form or by any means,
electronic or mechanical, including photography,
recording, or any information storage or retrieval system,
without permission in writing from the publisher. The book
is sold subject to the condition that it shall not, by way of
trade or otherwise, be lent, re-sold or otherwise circulated
without the publisher's prior consent in any form of
binding or cover other than that in which it is published and
without a similar condition including this condition being
imposed on the subsequent purchaser.

Cover design by Nicki Hayden
Printed by the Guernsey Press Ltd.,
Vale, Guernsey, Channel Islands.

A Strange Kind of Loving
Sheila Mooney

POOLBEG

To my grandson Oisín
with all my love

Neither weep nor laugh but understand

Spinoza

A Requiem for Edith

She waded in the cold brown water.
In between tedium and terror she
slowly walked until it closed above
her head. For one moment of clarity,
like a bird in flight, she saw
her life speed by and on she walked
until strange singing in her ears
played a last prelude before oblivion
bathed her in its nothingness. And so
the brown river rushed on and round
the naked body of a woman lifeless
as the moon, pale as its cold dead
light. Green weed is tangled in long
hair and these remains will go with the
brown rushing water spiralling slowly
in the current, as dead eyes scan a
cloudless sky searching for a spirit
damned in that act all nature spurns.
Death, the dark bird, rises and watches
as these remains are taken by the river
to disappear for ever in the open sea.

Contents

1 Tientsin, China

The long table was set for a dinner party: glistening silverware, sparkling cut glass, and the heavy damask table cloth touched the floor. Chinese servants pattered around setting big jugs of sake (rice wine) on the table. Chinese wind bells clinked and tinkled in doorways, keeping the evil spirits at bay.

Did they keep away the evil spirits though? I don't think so. The child hiding under the table was ten years old, already beautiful. Her name was Mary. She stole the sake every night, indeed became quite drunk on it. Later she was to become my mother and an alcoholic who, whatever she did, or said, always rated forgiveness! She was beautiful, witty and the soul of generosity. Even as a child I could love her and forgive her drunkenness. She was my beginning and part of her lives on in me.

My grandfather, Surgeon Captain John Lovatt Frazer, had retired from the Navy and was senior consultant to a big hospital in Tientsin. The Frazers had lived for many years in China where all of their eight children were born. Four boys and four girls, in that order. Grandfather had married an English girl, Eva Mary Kennett.

The children were all beautiful, bizarre, unstable and talented. No one had any idea why they were in China, where my grandfather ran a busy practice plus the hospital. My mother told me that the house was magnificent. The photographs show deep verandahs where my grandparents entertained during the hot summers. The house was staffed with Chinese servants: cook, coolies and Amah, the Chinese nanny to look after the children.

Strict protocol was observed on the main verandah. One end was my grandmother's and the other my grandfather's. Each entertained in their own fashion. Grandmother gave endless tea parties and had tables for bridge and mah-jong, a difficult Chinese game. Mah-jong is Chinese for sparrow, "the bird of a thousand songs," an irony one presumes, as the sparrow has only one song. Grandfather entertained his men friends, mostly doctors and surgeons from the hospital. They reclined on bamboo chairs or chaise longues, while indulging in serious smoking sessions, all the while fanned by a coolie who pulled the fan rope with his foot. Grandfather said this was a part of the Chinese culture. The men wore embroidered smoking jackets and little round sequined hats with tassels to prevent smoke discolouring their hair.

Ladies and gentlemen only came together for the glittering formal dinner parties for which my grandmother was famous. They ate mostly English food and any Chinese food was carefully supervised by my grandmother. Apparently the Chinese servants had been caught eating white mice and monkeys' brains, all discreetly smothered in bamboo shoots, and grandmother was not taking any chances. In the years prior to 1900 there were temples everywhere to different gods, of the Ming Dynasty, Taoist, Buddist, Islamic. Those were the days of rickshaws pulled by barefoot coolies, elaborate sedan chairs for wealthy mandarins. All the rich children flew beautiful kites and learned to paint and draw while still very young.

Chinese high caste ladies painted their skins as pale as alabaster and both men and women of the leisured classes wore their nails very long, to show they did no manual labour. Foot binding was still going on and the less talked-of breast binding. Grandmother said the Chinese had a love for what they called "lily feet." Tiny high-instepped feet were formed by binding the toes under the sole, from childhood. For centuries, since the pre-Christian era, Chinese women had plucked their eyebrows and painted their long nails. Clothes then were the pyjama-like *samo-foo*, tunic and baggy trousers with hair pinned on top in a tight top-knot. Much later this was replaced by the Manchu influenced *cheong-sam*, a tight-fitting dress with high Prussian collar and thigh-slit skirt.

Health-wise a great worry was tape worm. The Frazer children were forbidden to eat Chinese sweets. Grandfather was convinced that they caused the worm. He had a remedy called poo-chi pills, for tape worm and for diarrhoea and gastro-enteritis. My mother told me that her brother Harold passed a tape worm five feet long. Grandfather said it was very hard to destroy until the head was found. The treatment went on for months.

Soon tranquillity was to end. The year was 1900,

the start of the Boxer Rebellion. When the foreign legations in Peking were under siege and defended only by a handful of men, the Chinese commander-in-chief did not give the invading force the artillery that would have meant a speedy victory. Hence the massacre of men, women and children from the foreign states. The Boxers, a blood-thirsty hooligan rabble, set houses on fire and forced their victims into the fire at bayonet point. At Tientsin, my grandmother told me, the Boxers mutilated the women by cutting off their breasts and then left them to die on the city wall.

My mother told me how grandfather got a sick call from the local convent. He was taken with an attack of diarrhoea and arrived an hour late to find all the nuns had been brutally slaughtered by the Boxers and there were mutilated bodies everywhere. Although she was only a small child, she wandered out of the grounds. The street was full of dead bodies. Feeling that she was being watched, she turned round and a Chinese boy with a knife was standing behind her. She was wearing a lovely white fur cape and she thought he was going to steal the cape and then push her into the trench. She turned to him and said in Chinese, "I don't believe you would hurt a little child." He looked at her and ran away. She was a beautiful child. Had she been ugly, her fate might have been different. History records that eventually international force sent relief to the foreign legations in Peking, put down the Boxer rebellion which the Chinese Court had deliberately encouraged, and compelled the guilty Empress Tzu Hui to flee from China. The Frazers, too, had to flee China, terrified for their eight children.

As a child I was enthralled by the stories of China

which came alive in my mother's stories and in my perusal of many wonderful photographs. I was about seven when I wrote this little poem which my mother loved:

Broken Blossoms

The shaven-headed monks are standing
By the river Yangtze Kiang
Their saffron robes the breeze is swaying
They're saying good-bye to young priest Chang.
He is going to the mission very very far away
Children, they will learn of Buddah and the
way the Chinese pray, they will learn to
burn their joss sticks and that prayer
wheels turn and turn and that China
has a culture all the world could do to learn.
Slowly now the Sampans moving, time has come
To say farewell, high upon the hilltop clearly
Chang can hear the mission bell.
Chinese monks are standing sadly
Chinese boy must show no grief
Broken blossoms fall on river like
a lonely Chinese wreath.

It seems in bad taste to quote Confucius after a childish poem, but he was wise and would have seen the wonder of a child.

Confucius wrote:

The people should be cherished
And should not be down trodden
The people are the root of the country
And if the root is firm, the country
will be tranquil.

2

Riversdale, Co Roscommon —the Frazer Family

My grandfather had a property in the west of Ireland, so when the family had to leave China they settled in a beautiful house in Co Roscommon called Riversdale. Frazers had lived in the west of Ireland for centuries. My grandmother, née Eva Mary Kennett, was English and had a string of ancestors going back to the Plantaganets. A cousin, Lady Brigid King Harmon, lived in a big Georgian house called Rockingham on one of the other lakes near Riversdale. Peacocks strutted the lawns rattling their beautiful feathers and screaming if any one went near them. I do not remember Riversdale, but Maureen, my eldest sister, told me about it and how beautiful it was. It was a square Tudor house. Grandfather was so used to the Chinese servants that the family decided to bring them with them to Ireland. Had they been left in China, the Boxers would probably have slaughtered them because they had worked for the white ruling classes whose mansions were still standing.

There was a story told about Wang, the son of Amah and her husband, Chang Len. Because Wang was a rickshaw puller he would fret if he didn't pull the rickshaw so my grandfather would use him to run him to Sunday service up the stony boreen, the old man with his tall hat and his bible on his lap. He had a flick whip and a tip of it urged the coolie to run faster. The villagers must have been amazed, but I am told they got used to it.

Roscommon is the lake country of Ireland. Its lakes and the locks through which boats must pass, have been for centuries the waterways for trade, and for passenger travel to all parts of Ireland. It is also the land of the leprechauns and the little people and of the black turf that at one time supplied Ireland with most of its heat.

I do not remember my grandfather very well. I was only five years old when he died. But I do remember that I loved him. He was interested in me because I told him I had seen a leprechaun in the garden. He and I spent so long looking for it that I really believed in it and was terrified we might find it. Grandfather was a spiritualist and believed in the supernatural, including the fairies. Maureen told me that he was a lovable man. He was imposing, standing over six feet tall. He wore tweed suits which hung loosely on his gaunt frame. He was vague and easy-going, kind and amusing, this John Lovatt Frazer. He was of Scottish birth and it was assumed by many that he was the rightful Lord Lovatt Frazer. There was a lawsuit over the right to title involving Grandfather and his first cousin. Grandfather abandoned the case because of lack of funds to pay the lawyers in what promised to be a long drawn out battle. The vagueness of his nature also made him lose interest. So his cousin, a

7

well known artist, became Lord Lovatt Frazer. All the Frazers were gifted artists.

My grandfather was also a good doctor. My mother told me that once a man called to Riversdale with a badly gangrened leg. Grandfather cut it off immediately with a sharp knife, a bucket of disinfectant and a shot of whiskey for the patient. The poor man's screams were dreadful but he lived to be grateful.

I do not remember Grandmother Frazer very well either. I do remember that I hated her and I used to cook "mess-ups" for her and watch her eat them and hope that she would be sick. Maureen told me that Grandmother was as difficult as Grandfather was easy-going. She was imperious, dressed in a marvellous black clothes with a choker of fine lace round her neck to hide any trace of age. She wore a bonnet, both indoors and out, like Queen Victoria.

My Frazer grandparents had eight children in proper order, first four boys, Jack, Alec, Eddie and Harold. The girls, then, were my mother, Mary, Edith, Mona and Una. Eventually my grandparents separated. The boys kept the name of Frazer, and were brought up Protestants, while the girls spelt their name with an 's' instead of a 'z' and were brought up Catholics. They all lapsed, and became confused Christian Scientists. At least Grandfather and Grandmother made a pact over one important issue. They took it in turns to stay with their children at Riversdale. Each parent stayed with the family for one year, so their children were never exactly orphans though they told me they received no affection from either parent. However, they divided into two camps. The boys were closely united with each other, but ignored their sisters. The girls were almost too emotionally dependent on each other and they all adored their mother.

Social life in the country in those days was never dull, with endless tea parties, picnics and balls held in the great houses. I remember my grand-aunt Kate Frazer telling me of her trips to Dublin when she was a girl. Once every two years she and her sisters Lillah and Anna went to Dublin for the Season, to buy clothes and go to the winter balls. The barges that made the journey to Dublin were then drawn by horses and every night they stopped at one of the many little towns by the canal, finally winding their way into Dublin after nine days of travel.

Quite often yachts would stop where the canal led to Lough Key. Riversdale was about a quarter of a mile away from the lake. Then ladies and gentlemen in their yachting clothes would stop at the great houses for tea, or a drink or perhaps even dinner. There are so many lakes that one leads to another. Some have islands with ruins dating back to the 6th and 7th centuries. One island had a castle on it. Linking these lakes and leading all the way to Dublin were the canals Aunt Kate told me about.

My sister Maureen told me that when she and my brother Jack stayed at Riversdale as children, they frequently sat up in bed at night to listen to the music that thundered and crashed through the house. Sometimes it woke them. They did not know until many years later that there had been no musical instruments in the house. Grandfather believed in getting in touch with the other world.

One real horror story my mother told us years later was that when grandfather died, there was violent knocking from inside the coffin. The family put it down to his spiritualistic powers: he was trying to communicate with those he had left behind. I asked my mother, "why didn't you open the coffin?"

She was surprised at such a question. "How could we?" she replied, "the funeral was all arranged."

Though they divided their time between the two parents, the Frazers were united in a strange sort of way. Because they were all handsome and witty, they found each other more amusing than anyone else. When my grandmother was not in residence at Riversdale, she lived in Monte Carlo, where she had a villa. She spent her time gambling at the Casino. From Monte Carlo she would journey to Rome and gamble there. She spoke fluent French and Italian as well as Chinese. She also had a large luxurious flat in Dublin. There it was bridge. She was an expert and played for very high stakes.

My grandfather gave his four sons an excellent education; they went to an Irish public school, Aravon in Bray, Co Wicklow, where they graduated from the school's Officers Training Corps in preparation for joining a famous regiment. Three became commissioned officers in the 2nd Battalion of the Connaught Rangers. My Uncle Jack was killed early in his military career, my Uncles Alec and Harold advanced to rank of Captain. Uncle Eddie was the only one to become a Major in the Waterford Artillery.

Uncle Jack died before I was born. My mother described him as tall and good looking. He was a crack shot and many of the game he bagged in India, buffalo and antelope, adorned the walls of our home, Saintbury. He was musical with a fine tenor voice, very popular at parties, where he would sing standing by the piano, to his mother's accompaniment. He sported a monocle for his more risqué songs. My mother used say her greatest regret was that when her brother Jack left for the front, he came to say good-bye and she was too sleepy to get out of bed.

The second of the Frazer boys was Major Edward, my Uncle Eddie. A handsome man, great for the horses and the hunt. He never boasted that he was awarded the Croix de Guerre, the highest French award for bravery. He married a Miss Freda Murphy and retired to Co. Roscommon as a gentleman farmer. They lived in a beautiful mansion, Corodoo, standing on forty acres. They had two children, a boy, Ned, and a girl called Betty.

The third son was Captain Alec Frazer, my favourite, tall, dark and handsome, a crack shot. His name is still a legend in Oughterard, Co Galway. He married late in life, a pretty Irish girl and they had one daughter, Mary.

The youngest, Captain Harold Frazer, was perhaps the saddest. He too was a tall handsome man, a dreamer and a poet, not cut out to be a soldier. Sadly he did not cover himself in glory. The story goes that at the battle of the Somme in 1914 Captain Harold Frazer was told to order the men under his command, "over the top," out of the trenches to bayonet charge the oncoming Germans. Captain Frazer shouted his orders: "Men. Fix bayonets up and over. Charge!" But he himself charged in the wrong direction. He ran away screaming in terror and his men followed him. I never heard if there was a court-martial; all Uncle Harold ever said about it was, "I was born to be a poet and not a killer." Like the rest of the Frazers with one exception, his brother Major Frazer, my Uncle Eddie, Uncle Harold quickly ran through the money his father left him, mostly on drink and extravagant living. Eventually he ended up wandering round

London, sleeping in Salvation Army hostels, living the life of a tramp. Finally he died in St Kevin's hostel in Dublin. He used to steal money from the Salvation Army when he could. My brother Jackie said, "I put the few bob in Uncle Harold's pockets in the Salvation Army box." He went to an unmarked grave. He had never been loved by anyone.

The Frazer girls were Mary, later to become my mother, Edith, Mona and Una. My grandfather was adamant that he was not going to waste money educating them. They were all beautiful and in due course they were expected to marry whomever grandmother chose. Grandfather was not really interested in them. They were brought up by a retinue of ineffectual governesses and for a year they attended an academy for young ladies, in West Kensington, London to teach them to be ladies and precious little else. This was run by two spinsters, Miss Nimmo and Miss Tottle. I remember when I was seven years old, being very excited because my mother told me her former teacher was coming to stay in our house, Saintbury in Killiney. Miss Nimmo was old but upright. She wore her white hair piled high. All she said to me was, "child, kindly direct me to the library." I looked back and she was peering at the books through her lorgnette.

My mother was the eldest of the girls. She was beautiful but she already had a drink problem by the time she was eighteen. Edith was next. She too was beautiful. I never knew her, but she was a talented artist. Her life was a short one and ended tragically. At twenty-four she drowned herself in the river that ran through the grounds of her aunts', the Miss Frazers' house, Annagh, Co. Sligo. The waterfall at the main gates ran through the grounds and gathered in a still dark lake in the lower woods. Edith was found by the yardman, McConnell. She took her life because of her youngest sister, Una, who was then twenty and was slowly dying of tuberculosis. Una was in love with a young officer. He visited her regularly because he was in love with Edith. He wrote to Edith and told her that he loved her. It seems that Una came across the letter and in the manner of young girls was dramatically upset. Una died about three months later and my beautiful and kind aunt Edith put an end to her life in grief and guilt. An unfinished portrait of her sister Una was propped against a tree, by the river bank. Her father, when told of her death, said, "suicide is a noble thing!" The remark seems to derive from the old Chinese philosophy that life itself is not all that important.

In those days people who had taken their own lives were refused rest in consecrated ground. Edith Frazer was buried in a field behind Ardcarne churchyard in Co Sligo. Someone later erected a plain wooden cross. This churchyard was the Frazer burial ground. But there were very few Frazers interred there, as most of them died in different parts of the world. None of them felt any sentimentality about places of burial; all of them shared in the oriental indifference about what happens when the body is dead and the spirit has gone on. All the Frazer girls had an interest in the occult and the Frazer men, with the exception of Grandfather, had no interest in anything.

My aunt, Mona Frazer, was third in line of the four girls. She was probably the least beautiful but she was very attractive and full of life. Like all the Frazers she had a great sense of humour. After the death of her sister Una from tuberculosis and her sister Edith's suicide, she had a very bad nervous breakdown. Two years later she left the psychiatric hospital near Dublin. At that time, grandmother had a house overlooking the sea in Dalkey. It was called Shang-gri-la and was later to become an hotel.

Aunt Mona was accompanied everywhere by her nurse, a Miss Kelly. On this occasion the two were shopping in Kingstown, now Dun Laoghaire. Aunt Mona persuaded Nurse Kelly to take some time off and said that she felt really well and would like to go and visit her mother in Dalkey. The nurse agreed. It was half past three on a November's day. Aunt Mona, my mother told me, went to a pub and had a couple of stiff whiskeys and some of the anti-depressant pills. Then she started off on a walk down the West Pier. It was a cold day and the pier practically deserted. It appears she looked distraught, because a man followed her, wondering what a fashionably dressed and good looking lady was doing stumbling, half-running as she was. At the end of the pier she hesitated and then jumped into the freezing water. She could not swim. The man jumped in after her and saved her life.

When Grandmother was told she said, "My God— I hope she didn't have my new brown handbag with her." It was in the newspapers and the case came up in court. In those days an attempt at suicide merited one year in prison. The judge agreed to her lawyer's plea for clemency on the grounds that she was still being treated for depression and that the balance of her mind was disturbed.

Aunt Mona adored her mother and really gave up her life to being a companion help to her. Grandmother passed on to her daughter her own extravagance and love of gambling and the two together lost thousands at the Casino in Monte Carlo when they went to stay in Grandmother's villa there. Aunt Mona had a retinue of admirers; the one she would have married was Percy McDermott who was related to the McDermott Roe, Prince of Coolavin, an old Irish title. When Grandmother heard of her daughter's proposed marriage she immediately feigned illness as she did not want to lose her companion help. She loved none of her children except her son who was killed in 1914. Poor Aunt Mona, she was the one who dearly loved children. My mother gave birth to them and did not give a damn about them.

Having lost her chance of marriage to the man she loved, Aunt Mona stayed with her mother till the old lady died in her Dalkey home. By then she had gone through the money her father had left her, gambling and drinking. She was destitute. So she hung on to my mother, who supported her till the day she died. My father loathed Aunt Mona and she loathed him. He said she was a damned beggar. She had nursing experience. She had been a V.A.D. in 1914 and had four medals to prove it so the Irish Red Cross were glad to accept her. When she went to Spain with the Red Cross, during the Spanish Civil War, 1936-1939, he was delighted and more so when we got news that she had been arrested in Spain as a spy (she was not) and thrown into prison. I remember him laughing— he did not laugh easily—and saying, "that damned woman in prison; that's the best news I've ever had." After six months she was released. Her imprisonment was due to some stupid confusion and she was given a written apology and citation from the Spanish authorities. Aunt Mona said she slept on a stone floor and that there were rats in her cell. Maybe, but the Frazers always embroidered just to colour the canvas.

The surviving Frazers therefore suffered the losses of their brother Jack, killed in 1914, and their two sisters, Una who had died so young and Edith who took her own life.

3

The O'Sullivans of Cork

My father's family, the O'Sullivans, were steeped in Catholicism and made a far more prosaic and dully well-balanced menage. My father, Charles Joseph Major, was the eldest son of Sir Daniel Vincent and Lady Ellen O'Sullivan. My grandfather was Lord Mayor of Cork in 1881 and was later knighted by Edward VII for his charity to the poor of the city. He had inherited his firm from his father, Cornelius John O'Sullivan. He married an English girl, Ellen Scannell, and they lived in Arbutus Lodge in the fashionable Montenotte, Co. Cork. Then the mansion was the Mayoral residence. Arbutus Lodge was built in 1804. The house originally had three reception rooms on the ground floor plus the ballroom, kitchen, staff and billiard rooms in the basement. Upstairs there was a master bedroom en suite and five other bedrooms. The garden sloped down through three levels in front of the house with a kitchen garden and glasshouses. The view from the house in those days would have been over the Marina and Cork Racecourse on the far side of the river down to and including Blackrock Castle.

My father told me there was a staff of at least ten servants and that his parents drove in a coach and four with a pair of carriage dogs trotting behind the rear wheels. These were dalmatians and the Victorians called them "carriage dogs." My O'Sullivan grandparents had eight children: three sons, Dan, Charles (my father) and John, followed by five daughters, Josephine, Florence, Maud, Minnie and Edith. The children had sad and lonely lives because their parents died young. My father told me that when he was a very little boy, aged about seven, there was a terrible thunderstorm one night, so he was allowed to get into his father's bed. When he woke up in the morning he found his father cold, very cold, beside him. He had passed away in the night, aged only forty. His wife, Ellen, survived him by one year and died before she was forty. My grandfather's will said that in the event of his own and his wife's death, his brother Michael Joseph O'Sullivan should be legal guardian to his eight children.

Michael Joseph was as brusque as Sir Daniel was gentle. The children were all afraid of him and he had no use for them, or for anyone's children. He was disgusted, the more so because all of the girls were extremely plain. Known always by the awesome title of "The Uncle," he was a rich man, having made a fortune in Imperial Tobacco shares. He had a beautiful and unfaithful wife called Lily. She did have a loving heart though, and it is believed she would have cared for the orphans. "Too damn many of them," said The Uncle and duly put them all in boarding schools where they were left even for the school holidays. They loved Lily's occasional visits and hated and feared The Uncle—all except my father, who, as a child, stood up to him. His uncle liked that and an early rapport developed; The Uncle grew to love the boy Charles like the son he had never had. He had no use whatever for the rest.

The three boys were sent to school at Bonn in Germany and the girls to the Convent of the Assumption at 23, Kensington Square. The boys were bilingual in German and the girls bilingual in French as the Assumption was a French order. All the family had musical and artistic ability above the average. The Uncle himself had a good tenor voice and had played the lead in the West End production of *Rip Van Winkle*.

I never knew my father's eldest brother, Daniel Vincent O'Sullivan. I am told he was quite a famous cellist and a gentle cultured man. He died very young of tuberculosis. The third brother, John O'Sullivan, and Charles my father were both to become officers in the Connaught Rangers.

The Connaught Rangers started out as the 88th Regiment of Foot in the army list formed in 1793 and continued until they were one of the twenty-four infantry regiments disbanded in 1922. The Regimental colours of both battalions were laid up in St. George's Chapel, Windsor. The regiment was also called "the devil's own" for its daring. I remember my father telling me that when the regiment was stationed in Boyle, Co Roscommon in 1910-1911, the streets, the shops and the one hotel were daubed with the drab colour of khaki, as though by the hand of an artist. Sometimes bright red and the gleam of brass would flash through the dull scheme of things. That was when the military band in dress uniform would be on parade. Then the cheering crowds would come from their shops and houses to watch proudly as Ireland's greatest regiment went by.

Many soldiers of this famous regiment were soon to lay down their lives for the British in World War One. My father had a large picture done in oils in his library, named "Recruiting the Connaught Rangers." The Union Jack adorned the picture. It depicted an officer mounted on horseback and a little red-coated drummer boy, proudly playing a tattoo on his drum. Two big ragged and abject Irish tinkers walked beside them—new recruits! Father told me that the Irish tinkers made good and fearless soldiers. I wrote the following rhymed verse when I was twelve. To my joy, my father loved it and actually brought it down to his club, the Royal Irish Yacht Club, Dun Laoghaire, for his friends to read.

The Green And The Gold

Down in the heart of Roscommon
There's a story beloved of the old
'Tis the tale of the brave Connaught Rangers
How they brandished the green and the gold.

For those men were the pride of the country
And the mothers, their hearts beat with joy
At the sight of the red-coated majors
To the smallest and proud drummer boy.

Soon war clouds were dimming the bright skies
The lads, they were all sent away
To fight with the French and the Belgians
And keep the cruel Germans at bay.

While the poppies were growing in Flanders
From the blood of the bold and the fair
The mothers and sweethearts were weeping
All their thoughts with the boys over there.

Ah! 'tis said now that sometimes at twilight
When the shadows collect o'er the glen,
You can still hear the hoof beats of horses
And the bugles that called gallant men.

They died for their flag and their country
There are few of them left to grow old
We remember the brave Connaught Rangers
God bless 'em—the green and the gold.

(Green and gold were the regimental colours.)

The Uncle, and indeed my father as well, despised poor Uncle John, saying that he was a weakling who had never done much with his life. Later he married Aunt Dolly, but married out of his class. They lived in a little house in Brighton and had no family. I remember liking them both. Uncle John disgraced the snobbish O'Sullivans by driving a hansom cab round Brighton. I think from what I remember that I would have liked him better than my father.

The eldest of the girls, Josephine, was eccentric and dressed in a bizarre style of her own with big hats, feather boas and button boots. She was a brilliant artist and sets of her hand-painted silk table-mats and centre-pieces often adorned our dining table at parties. Aunt Josie, as she was known, had a habit of arriving when she was not wanted in the middle of a dinner party. She would let the family down just by dressing and acting in an extremely odd fashion. She lived her life out alone in Cork. She had never shown any interest in men but at the menopause she became too interested and would parade round the army barracks dolled-up in her finery. She died of pernicious anaemia in her early fifties. She was found dead in an attic room full of her paintings, in Cork city. Unlovable, unloved, she was the only one of his sisters that I saw my father cry for. They all died before him.

Next came Minnie. She became an Assumption nun and joined the order in the convent in Kensington where she had been at school, really the only home she had known. My father said it was "all that she was fit for, a miserable specimen!!" I gather that Minnie was very plain and had bad eyesight. Her decision to enter the convent caused my father to put a clause in his will—that ever-changing will—to the effect that, in the event of any of his daughters becoming nuns, they were to be disinherited. To enter the Assumption Order a girl had to bring in a substantial dowry. He did not want O'Sullivan money going to the nuns. Otherwise it was absurd, because we all detested convents and nuns.

My Aunt Florence, next in the O'Sullivan line, was an autocratic conservative Roman Catholic. She was a handsome strict woman, who married an unlikely candidate, a "nice little man," Fred Lyons, who was fond of the drink. She bore him two daughters and an invalid son, who lived out his short sad life in a wheelchair. I do not remember much about her except that I found her intimidating. She lived to have a comfortable old age and died fortified by the rites of the Church she had so strictly adhered to.

My fourth aunt, Maud, was a dear kind person. Although she was very plain, one forgot it because she had great charm, dressed beautifully and was a great hostess. She married an enormously rich and gregarious man, Oliver Piper, who provided her with every luxury. Like the proverbial ostrich with its head in the sand, she refused to acknowledge that he played around. Referring to sex she would say, "your uncle was very good about that sort of thing." She was a lovely person, but up to her eyebrows in traditional Catholicism. Sheelagh Graham, the well-known writer and journalist, a friend of my sister, Maureen, had an affair with Oliver Piper. She told Maureen that she was one of "many women." He left Aunt Maud so little money when he pre-deceased her that my father had to give her an allowance. She had one son, Dermot, whom she adored, and who was an amusing but weak character. She, who in her day had everything in the material sense, died in cold and miserable poverty. We heard that she had been sleeping rough in London's empty air raid shelters and in one of these she was found dead.

The youngest O'Sullivan sister, Edith, was a tiny little woman, known as Aunt Ned. I was really fond of her and she was such a wonderful pianist. She used to come and take me out when I was in boarding school. Sadly, I found out she was not fond of me and thought I was moody and odd, like my mother. So I switched off and stopped liking her. She used come from London to stay with us in Ireland and then write horrible things to the family about my mother. It takes all sorts to make a family! I suppose I am a part of all these genetically—the good, the bad, the spiritual and artistic. Well, Edith O'Sullivan, having lived in a lonely London bed-sit, finally died of cancer in the Bon Secours Hospital in Cork. At least the people she loved, my father's nieces and their families, were around her.

4

Love
and
Marriage

My father and mother met in Boyle, Co. Roscommon
in 1910 when his regiment was stationed there. The
officers and men of the Connaught Rangers were
greatly in demand for any one with an eligible
daughter; "the fishing fleet was out," was the way my
father put it. Mary Frazer and Charles O'Sullivan met
at the local tennis club and were drawn as partners for
the mixed doubles. After a set of tennis, the lovely girl
walked across the court and, holding out her hand,
said "thank you; drawn as partners for tennis and
partners for life." This was terribly audacious for that
time. Her tennis partner was, of course, intrigued and
later called to Riversdale and left his card. The
courtship began. "Did you love him?" I asked her
when she told me of their meeting. My mother
seemed surprised at such a question. "Oh, it was
nothing like that," she said, "I just knew it was
inevitable."

My mother was eighteen, my father twenty-eight.
My father proposed after calling twice at Riversdale

and they were married before the year was out.

My mother was the only one of the Frazer girls to marry. My father, then Lieutenant O'Sullivan in the 2nd Battalion The Connaught Rangers, was blonde and good looking. Grandmother Frazer had heard that he was a ward of a rich uncle Michael Joseph O'Sullivan. A good catch, she said. She refused to recognise her daughter's drink problem and told her that if she married early it would bring on her periods and cure her nerves. Lieutenant Charles O'Sullivan was chosen for my mother by Grandmother, though I often heard him say, "I was taken in by a pretty face."

Even though she had virtually chosen Charles O'Sullivan for her daughter, in her usual paradoxical way Grandmother led her family in deciding that the O'Sullivans were not only common but dull. This was because my grandfather O'Sullivan was one of the merchant princes of Cork city in 1881; he had made his fortune in trade. All the Frazer men were six foot tall, my father five foot seven. So Grandmother was always as rude as possible; she would deride my father and say "poor Charlie, he is very small," which he hated. It mollified her a little that Grandfather O'Sullivan had been titled. She tried to forget that his large income came from his extensive trade in feather beds!

Despite Grandmother's contempt for my father and the O'Sullivans, soon there was a bond between the two families. Her eldest son, Lieutenant John Irwin Frazer, my Uncle Jack, belonged to my father's regiment, the Connaught Rangers. During World War One, at the action of La Cour de Soupire, on 14 September 1914, my father was hit near the German trenches. Jack Frazer dragged him to safety and was killed. My Aunt Edith had painted his portrait in uniform. This hung in the large diningroom, among the family portraits, but in the place of honour on the wall to the right of the head of the long table and my father's chair. It was decorated with poppies and my father never sat down to dine without lifting his glass toward the man who had saved his life. Jack Frazer received posthumous citation. Even so, like the Capulets and the Montagues, the two families feuded for ever. With the exception of my Uncle Alec and my beautiful Aunt Edith, who was to die so tragically, the Frazers were forbidden to darken my parents' doors.

The Frazers apparently did not have enough money to pay for their daughter's wedding but it is thought that meanness was one more of Grandmother Frazer's foibles. So it fell to my father's guardian, Michael Joseph O'Sullivan, The Uncle, to pay for the wedding. As he and his wife Lily lived in Berkeley Square, they decided to have the reception in their home and the Nuptial Mass at Our Lady of Victories Church in West Kensington. This adjoined the Assumption Convent where my father's sister was a nun.

The bride was beautiful and her white satin wedding dress quite exquisite. My father told me that when his bride reached the end of the aisle to kneel before the altar, she handed her bouquet to her bridesmaid and drew her gown aside to reveal a pair of black and muddy boots. She had forgotten to change her shoes!

The honeymoon was spent at Ardleboden in Austria. My mother told me that on her wedding night, my father discreetly allowed her to go upstairs while he had a night-cap. When he reached the bedroom he found his bride out for the count. She was asleep sitting on the floor, propped against a chair with the fire singeing her boots, an empty whiskey bottle beside her.

Mary, my mother, found marriage difficult. She had never learned to cook and she had no idea how to keep a house. My parents' first home was in the Curragh, Co Kildare, where my father was stationed. At that stage he was living on a Lieutenant's pay and they could not afford a maid. They had a little house called Lough Brown Cottage. My mother was told that the Colonel's wife was coming to call, so on the day she dressed up in black as a parlour maid with a white cap and frilly apron. She opened the door to the Colonel's lady and said, "Good afternoon, madam, I regret that Mrs O'Sullivan is not at home."

The lady looked closely at her and said, "but are you not Mrs O'Sullivan?"

My mother's answer was "No, but I look very like her," and she shut the door. Of course the pathetic ploy was soon discovered but Mary O'Sullivan was forgiven. She was only eighteen and very beautiful and it was a good story to relate over dinner in the officers' mess. Another odd story she told was that on discovering that her husband liked lamb, she bought a whole side of sheep and hung it over the bath tub where it dripped blood and the nerves twitched in a way that both frightened her and made her sick. She was already expecting her first child.

The regiment moved back to Boyle, Co. Roscommon and my mother gave birth to her first child, a girl, Maureen Paula. She was born above a draper's shop, Miss Judd's, on the main street in Boyle, which runs straight and narrow in the fashion of Irish small towns. My father adored his little daughter and it seems the young couple were actually happy for a short time. But my mother grew restless and nervous and needed a break. My father requested leave and they moved to her parents' house, Riversdale. In the move she "lost" the baby. My father was frantic. They searched the house and the empty packing cases. No baby. At last my mother remembered that she had been storing wine in the cellar. There they found the baby, Maureen, peacefully asleep among the bottles. From then on, baby had a nanny—a series of nannies.

Mary O'Sullivan announced: "My next child will be born to the sound of bugles." Almost at the outbreak of World War One in 1914, she gave birth to a son, John Charles, my brother, Jackie, at Aldershot, England. He was actually born at reveille to the sound of bugles.

My father was seriously wounded at the front and invalided from the service. It broke his heart. He loved the regiment and used say "I loved the men, (the soldiers under his command) and the men loved me." He was to be racked with pain for the rest of his life. His right arm was shattered, the collar bone smashed to such a degree that the doctors could only recommend amputation. He refused amputation and, though the arm and his hand were totally paralysed, the nerve endings remained and sent out awful pain messages. My mother used knit woollen mittens to cover his poor bent fingers. He was always acutely self-conscious about his hand. He had the bullet that hit him mounted as a brooch and he gave it to me, but how could I wear the emblem of his suffering pinned to my coat? I hated it.

Mother could not face such suffering. She began to drink heavily and nervous breakdown followed nervous breakdown. When Maureen and Jackie were children they hardly saw her at all. Maureen said when she did come home "we did not know her or even like her, she was strange and eccentric." To make matters worse, my mother gave birth to another baby, a boy, Daniel Vincent. He was born in Dublin where she was staying with her mother. He arrived two years after Jackie and this upset her. She said she insisted on five years between each two children! This was a horror story. The nurse-midwife, Nurse Starr, who had attended her three confinements, gave the baby only water. She thought the milk was poisoned and though she loved the baby she starved him to death. My poor mother had another nervous breakdown and we were never allowed to mention the baby's name.

Whenever my mother became pregnant she wanted to move. There were six of us and every second one was born in England with five years between each two births, except for the baby who died. All the belongings, children and furniture were carted back and forth on the old mail boat. How the hell and why did my father put up with it? After all, he did have some part in the procreation side of things.

Soon my father and mother never spoke to each other except when they had to, or if they were having a row. My mother drank heavily all through her pregnancies. She told me that I was born steeped in John Jameson. We were living on the Strand Road, Merrion, in Dublin in a house called Cappagh. The house overlooked the long wet beach and on stormy nights the sea would come right up to the garden and wash everything away. It was 1920, at the height of the Troubles in Dublin. My father refused to have anything to do with the rebellion and continued, as he always did, wherever we lived, to fly his Union Jack over the house. He was well respected and there were never any incidents regarding the flag. Maureen told me that one night the Tans jumped over the garden wall and hammered loudly on the hall door. They were polite and apologetic when they heard it was the house of Major O'Sullivan, a British officer. The next day, at Merrion Gates, they dragged a man called Alan Bell off the tram and shot him against the wall. A black cross marks the spot. My mother had invited them in and treated them to tea and refreshments. Maureen told me that there were British soldiers billeted up the road and she and our brother, Jackie, would go to them for uniform buttons and souvenirs and also to the Tans who were equally nice to the children!

My mother dressed my brother Jackie like a girl until he was five. He had long black ringlets and broderie anglaise frocks. To make matters worse, he had to wear braces on his legs. He was a bit bandy and the poor little chap must have looked pathetic hopping along the Strand Road. Happily all of this had no ill-effects. He grew up to be a strong healthy man, a major in the British Army.

In 1921 I was born in Fitzwilliam Street in Dublin. My mother said that she had been tipped off that there was going to be an explosion, maybe the Four Courts. She liked a bit of excitement so she went into Dublin on the tram. Anyway, they blew up the Four Courts. She said she was blown five feet off the ground, conveniently opposite a maternity home, which was at 30 Fitzwilliam Street. It later became the Majestic Hotel and all those years later my daughter, Pauline, had her twenty-first party there. My father died just round the corner in the Merrion Nursing Home, my mother attended the Christian Science reading room in Merrion Square, I was to marry a dentist who had a practice in Fitzwilliam Street and I was to become the owner of No 26, a beautiful Georgian house. The good Lord drew the Fitzwilliam Street triangle for me. I am still walking that street regularly to visit my psychiatrist.

We left the Strand Road, Merrion, when my mother was pregnant with her fifth child. We went to live in a small house in Brighton while our new large house was being got ready in Bournemouth, where the fifth child, Patricia Mary, Pat, was born.

Then Nanny, Nurse Murielle Hardy, came into our lives. Indeed she brought us all up. In Bournemouth, we were living in a large and beautiful house called Kismet. I was only five so I do not remember too much about the house, except the baby screaming every night and Nanny pushing a cupboard against the nursery door. My Aunt Edith, (Ned), my father's sister, was staying with us. She told me the story years later. It seems there was loud knocking on the doors at night, especially the nursery door, and the baby and I would scream and scream. Nanny was terrified and blocked up the night nursery door every night. Electricians, plumbers, the lot were called in. Finally, Aunt Ned sent for a priest. There is a superstition that a priest who performs an exorcism usually dies, so a young healthy man was called in. I do remember my aunt walking along with a lighted candle and the priest sprinkling Holy Water to right and left while intoning the words of exorcism. The knocking did not subside. Six weeks later the young priest died! We had to leave the house so we all returned to Ireland. Years later I met an English couple in the Royal Irish Yacht Club, Dun Laoghaire. They had left a "haunted" house in Bournemouth; it was the same house,

Kismet. They could not live with the knocking on the doors at night!

I was destined to be the middle child in a hell called a marriage. Although there was plenty of money, I was shown no love and was pitifully neglected. I hated Nanny. She said, "Come on then and show me your clothes," and I showed her my two dresses, one with green boxes on it and the other with orange boxes. I thought them so beautiful. She said, "Is that all you've got?" It was all I had. She loved Pat the baby and she didn't love me. She used to take us to her fiancé's grave in Bournemouth's Protestant cemetery, St. Paul's; it was all mossy and springy. My friend Ray Castle and I used jump and jump on the grave to try and flatten him out and Nanny called us "nasty wicked children." Frank Millar was the fiancé's name and he had been killed in the 1914 war. Nanny said she was twenty-seven, but my father said "that damned woman will never see twenty-seven again."

My friend, Ray, was six. She had ringworm and her head was shaved so she always wore a black beret jammed down over her ears. I thought her very interesting.

Nanny forced me to eat all the things I hated. One day she gave me marrow. I hated it so much that I had to sit for an hour trying to wash it down with water. Nellie, the maid, quickly put some down the sink for me. Nannie was out of the room, so I threw a little more marrow under the table. She came back in and made me eat it off the floor. I got sick everywhere. I screamed and yelled and she smacked me with a cane on the back of my legs all the way up the stairs. I told my father and from then on he tried to look after me but he never talked to me. I don't know why, perhaps I was a nuisance. I was always afraid of him.

Those are my memories of Bournemouth when Nanny came. Because of the ghost and because my mother was restless and expecting another baby, we moved back to Ireland again. My father's guardian, The Uncle, died in London and his will left everything to my father, cutting off all the other O'Sullivans. My mother told me we were going to live in a huge house. When we got off the boat at Kingstown, as it was then, we walked up to the Royal Marine Hotel. I said, "Is that our new house?" My mother said it was and I, only five-and-a-half, replied, "Well, it's not as big as I thought it would be!" We stayed a year in the Marine Hotel while our new home, Saintbury, in Killiney, was being made ready.

5 Saintbury

I loved the house the first day I saw it and felt the house loved me. It was a beautiful old house built in 1898, long and sprawling, turreted at either end, nearly 400 feet above Killiney Bay and with a view over the Vale of Shangannagh and the north Wicklow hills. The house was built on rocks so that one came up steps to the hall door. From the front the house looked like an elongated bungalow. From the back it looked like a castle. In summer it was covered in Virginia creeper which turned a beautiful golden red in the autumn. The house stood on four acres and we had a vegetable garden, rose garden, orchard, tennis court and putting green. There was a lovely castellated summer-house and a beautiful plant called lobster's claw used climb over its portals in July. There were four conservatories for hot-house plants, grapes and peaches. I loved the fernery best. It was cool and green and little frogs used hop around in the moisture. In the front garden were two of the most beautiful willow trees whose branches touched the ground. To a child being under them felt like being inside a green tent.

At the main gates was the lodge where the gardener, West, and his wife lived. He was not the full shilling but he was a marvellous gardener. He worked the four acres of ground, including three large greenhouses. He called his wife "old Louisa Benedictus" (blessed Louisa) behind her back. He was afraid of her but liked to jeer at her. And he did hate Nanny; he thought, be it true or untrue, that she had turned the children against him. He loved us. So as Nanny was English, he called her "John Bull with the big red nose." We loved it when he shouted this at her! I saw West have a fit once and always hoped he'd have another because he leaped about and shouted and foam came out of his mouth. Then Mrs. West came and took West home. She didn't speak but put him sitting on down on a hard chair, with his feet in a basin of hot water and a cold cloth round his head. I always wondered how that cured him but it did and nothing was ever said about it. When anything had happened at home, like mother coming in disgustingly drunk or me being expelled from school, it was never mentioned, so that we all began to believe it had never happened.

Opposite the lodge were empty stables (we were all afraid of horses) and the garage with a turn-table for the car. As children we had great fun with this taking it in turns to spin round and round.

My father furnished the house with beautiful things, some carefully bid for at auctions but mostly priceless paintings, silver and antiques from his uncle's London flat. We had no electricity and the house was lit by gaslight, a much softer light than electric, and there were many lovely oil lamps. Our telephone was of the wind the handle and wait for the operator vintage! My father never got used to it. He always held it well away from him and shouted down the mouthpiece.

Huge antlers and heads of buffalo and antelope and various big game, shot in the Punjab by my Frazer uncles, looked sadly down from the walls in hallways. When I was a little girl I used feed these all before I went to bed at night, except the skeleton buffalos which had big black horns and were very frightening. We had an elephant's foot that gave off such a pong and a leopard skin rug sprawled in the alcove in the drawing-room; it still had its head. I thought it very sad. Some beautiful bearskin rugs— Chinese and Persian—covered the parquet floor as well and there were paintings by Monet, Sir John Lavery and Rubens. At one end of the large drawing-room, where we once danced over a hundred people, the entire wall was covered in an enormous tapestry of a sixteenth century fair and country dance. The lights were particularly beautiful pink and gold shells round the walls. At the top of the big staircase, whose brass stair-rods were polished every week, was a bronze cavalier holding a lamp, while at the bottom stood a reclining nymph holding a shell. The large windows and the very big one overlooking the panorama of Killiney Bay were draped in heavy blue velvet curtains held with gold rope with tasselled ends. My father had his own suite, bedroom, bathroom, smoking-room-cum-library. Here were all his regimental pictures and books and his large picture "Recruiting the Connaught Rangers," complete with Union Jack.

We all sat in my father's library because it was the only room with a fire and a wireless set. We only had a fire in the large drawing-room for parties. We were all avid listeners of the wireless set and Jackie, my brother, made a crystal set, a little box with earphones; we thought this wonderful. The large piano-pianola played a big part in my father's life. This stood in the big bay window of the drawing-room. It was made of beautiful cherry wood, had resonant bell-like tones and was regularly tuned. An equally valuable cabinet contained apertures for all the pianola rolls, operas, Strauss waltzes, even some lighter music. I think I learned my love and, indeed knowledge of music this way. No one could play the pianola like my father. He knew exactly when to play loudly or softly or indeed proudly by pressing the various buttons, soft, loud and fast and slow, so that he with his injured hand could enjoy the music he could no longer play and see the notes moving in time. I would put on my party frock and dance happily; then I felt close to my father.

The Protestant rectory was next door and ours was the only Roman Catholic house that Canon Barker visited! He and my father got on very well in a friendship based on mutual respect. Directly below Saintbury was another beautiful house, Kilmore, home of the late Doctor Bob Collis, born 1900, well-known pediatrician, writer and rugby international. His play, *Marrowbone Lane*, drew attention to workers' slave conditions in Dublin. He was keen on my sister Maureen but Hollywood wafted her away when she was only eighteen.

Our family Doctor, Joshua Pim, was three times tennis champion at Wimbledon. Neighbours included Katherine Tynan Hinkson, the poet who is probably best known for "All on an April Evening." Then the famous Hone family: Evie, Joseph and Nathaniel. Poet and biographer Flora Mitchell (Mrs

Jameson) lived nearby also. She wrote the book *Vanishing Dublin*. Mrs McAteer Parnell, wife of John Parnell, brother of Charles Stewart, lived in Sion House with her sister-in-law, Mrs McAteer. They were very old and wore blonde wigs. They gave a famous fancy dress ball every New Year's Eve. I went to it much later when I was seventeen, in a Victorian crinoline as "Alice Blue Gown." Apart from the living, famous shades of those who had passed over remained in the old Killiney mansions. John Millington Synge, 1871-1909, had lived in Glendalough House. John Blake Dillon, 1816-1866, leader of the Young Ireland movement, had lived nearby in Druid Lodge. A Father Healy, 1824-1894, a noted wit, was parish priest in the neighbouring village of Ballybrack. Count John McCormack had lived in Killiney as a young man.

We had quite a nice climate. The influence of the Gulf Stream brought moist air and favoured rhododendrons, fuchsia, blue hydrangeas and palm trees and all manner of semi-tropical flowers. It was said we had the smallest rainfall of anywhere in Ireland. Spring brought an array of daffodils. All that and my interest in the druid circles and ancient church made Killiney for me perhaps the only paradise I will ever know. Sometimes even now I feel my spirit return to Saintbury.

There was a secret passage which was very damp and dark. To get into it, you had to climb through the butler's pantry over the sink. There was a small white-washed room behind and a cave-like aperture in the wall. The passage went right through the walls of the house and into the garden through a tiny door in a crevice in the wall. Several of the houses nearby also had these passages because at one time Killiney was a great place for smuggling.

The house was so big that we all could live apart. My brother, Jackie, once remarked that, had the house been smaller, we might have got to know each other better. As it was, we all grew up caring very little for each other.

One of my father's hobbies was clocks. The house was full of them. I used be frightened at night when I heard them striking midnight. A man used come regularly to wind and maintain them. His other great love was the gardens where he spent hours. Because of his paralyzed arm and hand he could not do much except pruning the roses and shrubs. But he supervised everything. The garden was quite famous for its riot of flowers and shrubs and there were always people looking in the gate or asking if they might walk around. How sad for my father that my mother took no interest whatsoever, either in the house or the grounds, though she liked entertaining other Killiney wives to tea-parties held in the big drawing-room. "Damned old snob," my father called her.

She was always the centre of attention, very amusing, a great and sometimes cruel raconteur. One would hear peals of laughter and know it was directed at some unfortunate guest. I learned how to divert her from this jeering. She would say in front of a crowd of people about me or one of my sisters "the dumplings are boiling over"—we were all well endowed—and whichever one of us was in question would be scarlet with embarrassment. When she did this, I would throw in something like, "did you hear the awful thing so and so did?" and she would seize upon that and leave me alone. I was the only one who learned how to cope with her and even then not all that much!

My mother had thought there were twenty bedrooms in the house. She was annoyed to discover there were only nine, with big dressing rooms off the two master bedrooms. The servants' quarters were a large flagged kitchen, scullery and a big larder with cold stone counters. No fridges in those days. The three servants' bedrooms were off the kitchen. Strict protocol was observed with the servants. Cook, parlour-maid and kitchen-maid, all ate in the kitchen. The charwoman stood in the scullery for a snack lunch. The gardener, if he did not go home to the gate lodge, ate in a shed, known as "the cat house" because Minnie the cat always had her kittens there. Nanny ate in the day nursery with the children and the kitchen-maid waited on the nurseries.

My father used say about Nanny: "that damned old woman never stops ringing the bell." Nanny entertained other nannies and the children they were caring for. There was great snobbery about who had the best nursery and gave the best teas. The nannies all wore the uniforms of whatever college they had trained in and a badge on their hats. The afternoon walk took about an hour to get ready. A perfect pram, in summer a canopy, a beautifully turned-out baby and an immaculate toddler who had to hold the handle of the pram and walk beside Nanny. Older children were allowed walk in front of the nannies and prams. We were never allowed to run. We, my sisters and I, were always threatened with "I'll tell your Daddy" and Nanny did tell. A few words from him were enough; he never hit any of us. Mother didn't count; she let us do what we wanted. She alternated between making free with the servants and then turning haughty on them. None of them stayed long and my mother was always ringing up the domestic agencies for maids. We had quite a varied assortment and an awful lot of stealing. I remember once going to the large press to get out my summer clothes to find they had all gone!

Our diningroom, like the drawingroom, was large and very cold. The only heating was the one coal fire in the smoking room and the anthracite stove in the diningroom was inadequate. The bedrooms just had electric heaters. The diningroom had a character of its own. It did not seem pretty or lovely like the drawingroom. To me it felt a bit grim. Sour-faced O'Sullivan ancestors stared down coldly and unsmilingly from their ornate frames. It was a little like the Chamber of Horrors at Madame Tussaud's. Over the mantelpiece was Sir Daniel, my grandfather, in his mayoral robes and on his left my grandmother resplendent in green. To grandfather's right his father, Cornelius John, with beetling white eyebrows, and eyes that seemed to follow one everywhere. All round the room were these unsmiling faces. It was hard to imagine any of them laughing or having fun.

Suspended over the middle of the long diningroom table was a large red-shaded light. Father sat at one end of the table and my mother at the other. He would pull the shade light down, as he said to my mother, "so that I can't see your damned silly face." She was never short of an appropriate riposte. There was really no conversation; all was silent except for the odd belch from mother. The tension was terrible.

My father and mother were *both* snobs. Everything had to be done correctly. The parlour-maid wore blue until the evening, when she changed into black and white. Because of the constant turnover of cooks, the food was awful. But as long as the table was set properly with nice china and silver cutlery, my parents overlooked a lot. Proprieties were always observed. Finger bowls arrived with the after-dinner fruit. Once a guest drank from his and so did my father to save him embarrassment. We were not allowed gossip with the servants. My father was quite adamant about that; he said that if one got familiar with them they didn't work as well. I grew up at the end of an era. It was getting harder to find staff and, sadly, gracious living was beginning to disappear.

6

Childhood

Even when I was growing up, all my father ever said to me at dinner was: "did you come home on the bus or the train?" or, "was the bus very crowded?" I answered yes or no and that was the evening's conversation over! Every night my father did a tour of the house to see who was in or out. If we were in he would put the bolt and chain on the hall door. If we were out he would lie awake until we came in. If we were too late, say eleven-thirty, there would be a telling off the next day. It ruined everything for me knowing he was awake listening and waiting.

My father took charge of me. My mother didn't bother and Nanny didn't like me. When I was small my cot was in his room. I hated it. He thought it was a great privilege! He snored and I was so nervous of him that if I wanted to spend a penny in the middle of the night I would wake him up and say, "May I sit down please, Dad?" We all had chamber pots. He used to put his dressing-gown over one side of my cot so that I couldn't see him having a pee. One night I stood up to watch and he clobbered me on the head with a heavy book. I was in disgrace and my cot was moved upstairs.

When I was five I had a bantam cock, Henry. He was beautiful and he followed me everywhere. One day I found him dead, eaten by rats, my first ever death experience. I will never forget the shock and horror. If only grown ups realised how strongly children love and hate too.

I was six when Sir Frank Benson's company came to Dublin. They were doing *A Midsummer Night's Dream*. Various dancing classes had been auditioned looking for a little girl to take the part of the fairy Mustardseed and also to dance solo in a yellow spotlight while Oberon and Titiana slept on stage. I was chosen. I was a pupil in the Leggatt Byrne School of Dancing in Baggot Street and already showing some talent. During rehearsals I was afraid of Bottom, the man with the donkey's head but I didn't say anything, just went on with my dance. The big night came. My dress for playing Fairy Mustardseed was yellow and I had gold wings. I felt really happy as I danced; it was as if I really was in fairyland. Other little girls were dressed as fairies, Peaseblossom, Cobweb and Moth. Suddenly, the man with the donkey's head appeared. I was terrified. I screamed and ran off stage. The audience loved it and Sir Frank Benson was not a bit cross. He said, "Little one, you were a real fairy!"

I remember Mother promising to take me to a Mrs Carr's cottage to see the "miraculous picture." I was only six and I wanted to go but at the same time I was afraid. Mother said I would have to put up with the smell off Mrs. Carr if I wanted to see the picture. We went down to the village and Mrs. Carr let us in. It was a dark room, she was a big fat woman, and the pong off her was awful. The picture of the Sacred Heart was over the fireplace. I was reassured, but our hostess said, "Oh no dear, it's not an ordinary picture at all, you have to keep looking at it and He will close His eyes and open them." I looked up at the picture again. The eyes were open but suddenly they shut. I ran out of the house and up the road as if all the devils in hell were after me. They should have told me that it was one of those pictures with the eyes superimposed on the closed lids to give the necessary illusion.

About the same time our parish priest, Father Potter, died. He had been a martinet. He used walk in the summer evenings along the Bray end of Killiney beach. Here he sought out the courting couples and was known to thrash out at the bushes with his stick. We got thunderous sermons about courtship and hell. It was hard to imagine him dead. He also could be amusing and for all his carry on it was often "tongue in cheek" with a twinkle in his eye.

So, when my sister, Pat , and I heard that everyone was going into the parochial house to have a look at Father Potter, we decided to pay a visit. I rang the bell and the housekeeper came out. She brought us into the bedroom. Laid out on the bed was a thin waxen creature. He had died of cancer. He had on his Benediction outfit. For this ceremony, the priest wears ornate vestments, all gold and shiny, coming on to the altar with a mitre, akin to a bishop's, on his head. The mitre is removed and handed to an altar boy before the ceremony begins. This was Father Potter's heaven outfit. He was holding a huge cross to whack the devil with if he should meet him on the way! I had a morbid preoccupation with death and was confused that Father Potter went down into the ground in a box and at the same time managed to fly up to heaven or to purgatory for a week or two.

While my father's first love was for Maureen, he must have been fond of me. When I was seven he started to try and improve my musical appreciation. I showed promise at the piano and, even then, was adept at a small piano accordion. We went to all the operas, but except for fairy-like things like *Iolanthe*, I was bored. And all these outings were silent. We used to dine at Jammet's in Nassau Street, and the Royal Hibernian. I suffered agonies of shyness, because even at that age I knew how badly dressed I was. A navy gaberdine, red beret and wellington boots! Through a child's eyes, those places were very grand and so were the stylish people dining there. Later, when I grew older, I have fond memories of Jammet's, the beautiful Edwardian decor, red plush wallpaper, beautiful oval Cheval mirrors. All the circular tables were dressed in plain heavy white linen table cloths and napkins. No plated cutlery, but beautiful heavy silver and silver candlebras. Each waiter had four tables and, of course, the waiting was impeccable. People who were regulars always asked for their favourite waiter. I remember Paddy and Victor. The cuisine can only be described as pure artistry, complemented by fine wine. Bacchus would have been quite satisfied in this gourmet's paradise.

Much as I loved Saintbury it was a very cold house and I suffered from terrible and prolonged coughs. Later in life it was confirmed by x-ray that I had had very bad primary TB. I used cry at night with the pain of coughing. My father would tell Nanny to rub my chest with camphorated oil and then cover it with orange-coloured thermogene wadding. My sister, Pat, developed tubercular glands in her neck and had to go through the painful procedure of having the fluid drained out of them. Two glands were surgically removed. Another misery for me was that all my back teeth were rotten by the time I was seven; I had four abcesses. I was taken to a Mrs Sterling in Fitzwilliam Square. She had an old foot drill and she hurt me so much that she put me off dentists for life. I had eight teeth extracted under a great dose of ether and the awful experience of having a bag forcibly held over my face.

My younger sisters, Pat and Betty, had beautiful long hair, Nanny's pride and joy. It was discovered that I was walking with nits and so my hair was all hacked off. I cried over that and I had to go about with awful peppermint-smelling lotion on my head. No one showed me any affection. When I was little I lavished my love on my teddy bears and later my series of dogs! Once, I was crying a lot and my father for the first time put his arm round me. He said, "don't cry or I'll cry too." I was frightened. I did not under-stand him when he was like that. I would rather have had him cross with me. So I tried to keep him cross. Mother told me she had never cried. I never saw her cry. She said she didn't know how but that I would do all her crying for her.

Next for me three governesses in succession. One of the smaller downstairs rooms was painted a cheerful yellow and fitted out with table, chairs and a blackboard. I hated having to give up my freedom and used hide up a tree in the garden every morning.

The first governess was a Miss Kissane. She had black hair and wore hand-crocheted jumpers. She could not make me interested in learning. My father said she was "no damn good" so he fired her. The second was Miss Marjorie Britten. I liked her and she taught me lots of poetry. The very first poem was Robert Louis Stevenson's "I had a little shadow." She found out I had a flair for drawing and she gave me a beautiful, real grey rabbit. But although my father said she "brought me on well" and "was a very good teacher," she had BO and as she had to pass my father's room to get to our schoolroom, he said "I can smell that damn woman all through the house!" He fired her and I missed her and was sad. When I grew older I heard she had written books and children's stories. The third of my governesses was a pretty girl, Miss Kathleen Hand. I decided to be really bad because I missed Miss Britten and the new girl could not control me at all. My sister, Maureen, went to be screen-tested for a part in a film called *Song of My Heart* and Miss Hand went to be tested too. My mother said she had a cheek. Maureen was much better-looking and got the part out of a hundred girls. Miss Hand left, but not before she had prepared me for my first Holy Communion and—horrors—my first Confession.

I was seven. At Confession when the priest opens the shutter the penitent says "bless me Father for I have sinned." I had given this some thought. I went into Father Grogan's box because he was the nice priest. He opened the shutter and I said,"this is my first confession, bless me mother for I have sinned," because I wanted my mother blessed and not my father. The priest was laughing and he explained things to me. Next day was my First Communion, the early Mass, eight o'clock and fasting from midnight. Miss Hand took me. She gave me a medal on a chain and I had a white dress and veil. I felt very holy. I sat out in the cowfield talking to Little Jesus and I made daisy chains for Him and hung them on the bushes. I thought he had taken them because next day they were gone. My mother said not at all, the cows ate them, and I really hated her then.

My younger sisters Pat and Betty spent this time in the day nursery with Nanny. Pat was five years younger than me and Betty eight. Maureen was ten years older than me, so we seldom met. I was eight when she left for Hollywood at the age of eighteen. Before then she had been a boarder at the Sacred Heart Convent Roehampton, and then at finishing school in France, ending up at Boxmoor in the south of England learning all about poultry, farming. Her interest in hens did not last! So I had seen very little of her.

I remember when Maureen left home. She had been invited to a dance in the Metropole. She did not want to go, but my mother said "go—you never know who you might meet!" How right she was! Maureen was eighteen and beautiful, fresh from finishing school. She wore white and was noticed by director Frank Borzage. He was looking for an Irish girl to play the ingénue in *Song of my Heart*, in which Count John McCormack was to star. Borzage sent over his card. She went for a test and out of a hundred candidates she was chosen. The film itself was a simple story about a young man with a beautiful voice who falls in love but his beloved, Eileen Joyce, dies. Many of McCormack's most touching songs were immortalised by this film, "The Rose of Tralee" and "The Little Boy Blue" among them.

My father had just returned from his regimental dinner in London. He had a surprise: tickets for Maureen, my mother and himself to go on a world cruise. He tore the tickets up and he did not stand in her way. He told her that if she kept her head and her religion she would succeed. I think her leaving really broke his heart. So at eighteen with our mother as chaperone (some chaperone!) she sailed across the Atlantic and out of my life. Maureen still says that she believed her father loved her more than anyone in the world. He knew what a great opportunity this was for her and that she had to go to the States. She told me when she was thirteen and got her first period, our mother was jeering as usual—one of mother's beastly habits—and she went to her room to cry. Father came to comfort her, but she found his words and gestures more than she could cope with. It was understandable; my father was lonely and withdrawn. My mother was rarely sober and his daughter made all his dreams come true. Apart from good looks, she had charm and a most wonderful manner. Despite her affection for her father she stayed away in Hollywood for fourteen years. She escaped from the drama that nearly destroyed me and certainly left its mark on each one of us.

Jackie was seven years older than me and he was away at the Oratory School, Reading, and then with the British Army in Palestine. I hardly knew him. Jackie was good to me before he was posted abroad and when, later on, I was sent in turn to an Irish and then two English convent boarding schools, he used come and see me. I was very proud of my soldier brother. When he came home he was moody but had inherited the Frazer sense of humour and could be great fun. The rest was all his father. He was cast in the mould!

7   Sion Hill

I saw my father looking at books with "Convent School" written on them and I was terrified. He said, "how would you like to go to Sion Hill?" This was a big convent boarding and day school in Blackrock, Co Dublin. The nuns, Dominicans, wore white with black veils and a cord round their waists with very long rosary beads threaded through. So I was packed off to Sion Hill! The senior girls teased me dreadfully. "So you're Maureen O'Sullivan's sister, you don't look like a film star." Maureen was then acting in the Tarzan films and was well known. I cried myself to sleep every night. I brought "Father," my teddy bear with me but kept him hidden in case the girls would jeer at me. I used take him out of the cupboard at night and tell him all my worries. We wore black—so depressing —and black veils in chapel. There was no talking at meals and a nun would read boring passages from *The Letters of St Augustine* or writings by St Theresa of Avila.

We had classes in a building separate from the

convent called "Melrose." My father would not let me learn Irish. He even paid a government grant for me in order that I should not have to learn it. So I sat at the back during Irish, drawing or just messing. I did pick up quite a bit of Irish just from listening to the others. Academically, I was hopeless, especially at Maths. I simply could not grasp them. Mother Gerald would explain three times with controlled exasperation and then she would say, "now you do it," and I had no idea. There was a block in my brain! She would put her head in her hands and say, "Ave Maria gratia plena." I shone only at composition, music, dancing and drama but was told, "none of these will earn you a living." Camogie was compulsory, like hurling and rougher than hockey. I hated it.

There was great emphasis on Irish dancing. I loved it. Here I must add that my father was anti-Irish and wanted me brought up a West Brit; at eight years of age I was. I was frightened of Sinn Feiners and people who said "up Dev!" (de Valera was then the Taoiseach). Emer de Valera, the Taoiseach's daughter, was in the senior school. When the big Irish dancing competition arrived I knew I could win. Emer and I came through as the last two for the reel and the hornpipe. The hornpipe is very difficult and I was young to have mastered it. I knew that I couldn't go home to my father with a cup for Irish dancing. He'd be cross and possibly say, "I've no use for that ugly stiff dancing," which he often did say. I did the unforgivable in Irish dancing, stared down at my feet so I didn't win. I felt very sad. When Eamon de Valera visited the school, he addressed us all in the big assembly hall. At the end I was the only one sitting for the national anthem, all to please my dad! My mother would come on Sundays to visit. I dreaded it. She was often drunk and I was afraid my friends would see her. My sister Pat also came for a term to Sion Hill to make her Holy Communion but she was always crying and didn't settle at all.

At the end of a year, my father decided I was talking with a Dublin accent, which was not on. He called to see the Mother Prioress and told her of his intention to send me to an English convent. She was very upset and kept saying, "Major O'Sullivan, I don't understand how you can send her away and to England too." But that was it; my sojourn in Sion Hill was over.

8 Holidays at Annagh

Before I was sent away to school in England I was looking forward to one bright spot, our holidays. When we were children, we went to our grand-aunts, the Miss Frazers. They lived in a rambling old house called Annagh, six miles outside Sligo town. The aunts, Kate and Anna, had not moved with the times at all. Kate was the bossy competent one, Anna was a pretty Dresden-type old lady. I didn't know it then, but she was already amiably senile. They both wore fusty Victorian clothes and on Sundays hats piled with fruit and feathers. Kate ran the house with the help of her housekeeper, Beatrice. She baked and made jams and marmalade.

I loved Annagh. It was pre-Victorian and everything in it was old and dusty like the home of Miss Havisham in *Great Expectations*. The house was surrounded by acres of land. Beside the main gate was a waterfall and the brown water wove its way down the sloping garden to the dark wood, where it rose to be a reasonably deep lake. It was dark down there and the only light was an eerie dappled sunlight through the branches of very old trees that still dressed for spring in their fresh green foliage. In the garden was a wonderful tree, known as the umbrella tree because it formed a perfect circle, the branches touching the ground. There was even a wooden table and stools inside that circle and we often had afternoon tea there. When the aunts made an occasional trip to Sligo they got into the village hire car with fear and trepidation and the driver wasn't allowed to do more than twenty miles an hour. They both wore motoring bonnets with a veil tied over both hat and face to protect them from the dust. Otherwise, McConnell, the hired hand, drove them in the pony trap.

The aunts were bigoted Protestants and did not like Roman Catholics. My uncles, Alec and Harold, had both become Catholics and then changed back. They were afraid of being cut out of the aunts' will. My uncle Eddie, Major Frazer, who owned a big house, Corodoo in Co Sligo, was a frequent hanger-on at Annagh and a good Protestant too! He was a great man for the hunt and professed to be a gentleman farmer. Uncle Alec and Uncle Harold, both Captain Frazers, were nothing, careerwise. They were ex-army, another pair of "hangers-on." Uncle Harold lived with the aunts.

Our family party consisted of my mother and her sister, Auntie Mona, Nanny and the two little ones, my younger sisters, Pat and Betty and Mrs West, our gardener's wife, to look after me. I hated her! She was 6ft 2ins, the daughter of a Metropolitan policeman. Mrs West was respectable and clean and hardly ever spoke. I don't think she knew how to smile. I had to sleep in a four poster bed with her. Oh, how I hated it. She sat upright on a hard chair looking straight ahead while I undressed. At bedtime she spoke a little. She pointed to my bundle of clothes and she said, "Fold them. Skirt goes over the back of the chair. Put your knickers under your blouse in case McConnell (the yard man) comes in with the turf." Then, bathroom. Mrs West spoke again. "Wash your neck." Ablutions finished, I pattered in in my long nightgown. "Come here," she said, and she plaited my hair so tight that it hurt. She pointed again. "Prayers, and stay on the left hand side of the bed and don't move till morning."

The four poster smelt damp and musty and the linen sheets were hard and scratchy. The canopy and curtains were a very faded pink-and-gold damask. I'd hear Beatrice the housekeeper say, "That old bed's seen birth, life and death, not to mention a bit of carry on." I asked Auntie Mona, "What's 'carry on' in a bed?" She took a fit of laughing and she said "Go and ask your mother, I'm only a maiden aunt." I still didn't know, but "birth" was easy I thought: the ginger cat, Sligo, had probably had her kittens in the bed.

It was high up to climb in. I hugged "Father," the bear who was the father of little Edward, my other bear. I loved them and could tell them things. Mrs West lowered the light. It was gaslight, very dim. She, undressed under her coat (I peeped) and folded her clothes. I watched to see if she would hide her knickers. She did. She put them under her cardigan! I wondered what was so rude about knickers that they had to be hidden? In the bed it was awful. She was awake, I could tell. I wanted to turn over and I wasn't allowed. I waited till her breathing was all in and out and I timidly turned, just a little. My foot touched her nasty damp cold feet, a toenail like a parrot's claw. I screamed. She woke. "Behave yourself miss. If you want to use your commode it's under the bed." I didn't want to use it, but I wanted to see if I'd got the one with the gold rim and the poppies that I'd asked Grand-aunt Kate for. I hopped out of the bed and nearly fell it was so high. There was the commode. Nannie said it was vulgar to call it a jerry or a po. It *had* poppies with green leaves and a gold rim. I looked inside. There were more poppies in the commode. I sat on it; it was too big for my little behind. I pushed it back under the bed and had another good look at the same time. Mrs West had a commode on her side but ha! it was a plain white tin one, what my mother called "a servant's commode."

Was Mrs West a servant? She seemed too grand and she and Nanny didn't eat in the kitchen, they ate in the day nursery. I asked Beatrice, the housekeeper, and she said Mrs West and Nanny were upper-class servants. She laughed and said "Them two wouldn't call the bloody Queen their aunt." I told my mother when she was sober and she said, "Don't talk to Beatrice, she is the height of vulgarity." I wondered what that was. But I was so glad that awful Mrs West was really only an upper-class servant and that she had a servant's commode under the bed.

Beatrice, the housekeeper, was tall and very dark. She said she had Spanish blood and she had a moustache. Auntie Mona said she could be half a man! That was very interesting. I thought about that.

When I woke in the morning Mrs West was up and dressed, with a lovely apron and her hat on, dead straight. I asked Nanny why Mrs West wore her hat in the house and Nanny said, "because she don't want to look like Ellie and Essie Gray, them two skivvies." They were sisters, Essie was our parlour-maid and Ellie was the nursery maid. Nanny was very much in awe of Mrs West. Everything was, "oh yes Mrs West" and "of course Mrs West."

Well! I was covered in spots all over. Nanny had a look at them. She said it wasn't measles. "It's the bites, that bloomin' dog Jock is alive with fleas." Jock was my grand-aunt's dog. He was a nice poor thing; it wasn't his fault. Nannie looked in the four-poster bed and she found a flea. I asked my mother why Mrs West wasn't bitten and she said, "She's so sour not even the fleas would bite her." I asked Auntie Mona why Beatrice had a moustache and she laughed and said "She's probably got more than a moustache." I told my mother and she said, "That was a terrible thing to say to a child." I didn't know what they meant.

McConnell was a grumpy big man. He had no teeth and he said "Me gums are that strong I could bite wire." My Uncle Harold said he was "a thick—a son of the soil." He looked after the pigs. He must have been a very low-class servant because he ate his lunch in the shed in the yard. I asked him. I said, "McConnell, are you a very low class servant?" He went red and got very cross. Nanny said I shouldn't have said that.

There was another maid called Mary. She was only fifteen. Beatrice said she had a "want." "What is a want?" I asked. Beatrice said, "It is a man." I told Nanny. She went red and said, "You wicked child, I'll have to tell the Major" (my father). Nanny did tell him and I saw him laughing behind his *Irish Times*. I wondered why he was laughing.

Beatrice used go into Sligo in the pony and trap with McConnell. I heard Nanny say to Mrs West, "There's funny business going on with those two." I told Auntie Mona and she said, "You'd need to be funny to kiss a woman with a moustache" and she kept laughing. My mother said "My God, Mona's vulgar!" Beatrice brought back a huge box of Keating's flea powder. I was allowed to powder Jock, the dog. I told him, "I had nits once, they look different from fleas but they bite just as bad." Mrs West put Keating's powder all over the four-poster bed. She got a chair and stood on it to powder the canopy. She even stripped the bed and powdered the blankets and sheets. Then the terrible thing happened. She said, "Those two old teddy bears of yours will have to get a going over." Father, the big bear, was father to "Little Edward." Little Edward was very delicate and had such a sad face. She went over and picked up my teddy bears. I screamed at her, "You leave them alone, they're mine. I hate you. My mother says even the fleas don't bite you cause you're so sour." Mrs West went white. She snatched away my toys and left the room. Auntie Mona, who was always on the side of children, came in. She said, "Don't upset yourself darling, she's a horrible woman. Auntie will get you your bears." She got them back for me.

That night Nanny said I had to have a bath in Condey's Fluid. Pat and Betty were bathed in it too. I liked it because first of all it was blue and then it turned pink. It was for our flea bites. Mrs West didn't speak one word that night. She was on her knees a long time saying her prayers. I was sorry for God. He must have been bored stiff.

My Grand-aunts had a green parrot called Jacko. He used shout, "where's Kate, where's Anna." He said a lot of rude things too and the cage was covered up to keep him quiet when the Archdeacon called. One day when the Archdeacon came to tea I lifted up a corner of the cover on the cage and Jacko started saying, "Dan, Dan's a dirty old man." Aunt Kate was cross and rang the bell for Beatrice to take Jacko to the kitchen. My mother said she was glad that Jacko was rude. She said, "That old fellow, the Archdeacon, is a pain in the you know what!" I didn't know what she meant.

The waterfall at the main gates was beautiful, all white and frothy and it made a singing noise. My Uncle Harold, who was a poet, told me that the water sang to the trees and the trees danced and swayed to the song. It was brown, that water, and very cold. It went down to the lower lake which was surrounded by trees. I remember paddling in the brown water looking for crayfish under the stones and then getting frightened in case the ghost of my Aunt Edith would come floating down the river, white with green weed entangled in her hair, like the Lady of Shalott.

Aunt Kate had a queer sort of gramophone. She called it a phonograph. You had to keep winding the handle round and round. Grand-aunt Anna used to dance the cake-walk for me; she lifted her knees so high I could see her drawers. Aunt Kate said, "The child will cause Anna's death." My mother replied, "She might as well die doing the cake-walk as anything else."

Time stood still in that old house. The aunts had not moved with the times. Proprieties and manners, music boxes and the most marvellous scrapbooks, full of Victorian Valentine cards and birthday and Christmas cards. Aunt Kate told me when she and Aunt Anna were girls there was not much to do in the country and on wet afternoons they attended to their scrapbooks. She showed me the cards they used at dances where the girls wrote down the names of the man reserved for the next quadrille, cake-walk, waltz or schottische, the dances of their young days.

There was a pretty cottage piano. Over the yellowed keyboard was a lattice-work of faded blue silk and not one of the keys sounded a note. I asked Grand-aunt Anna, "Why doesn't the piano play?" She said, "It's like me, dear, it's too old to play any more; that piano died a long time ago." That was the first dead piano I had ever seen. The furniture had funny names: a tall-boy, bureau, cabinets, loveseats and little ornaments called "whatnots." Even the little hand-crocheted doylies over the backs of all the chairs were called anti-macassars. Aunt Kate said "When we were girls, the men put so much pomade (hair oil) on their hair; they used macassar oil; that is where the doylies got their name." All the chairs had ruffles on the legs. Beatrice said, "Only rude chairs showed their legs according to Miss Kate." She was laughing. It seemed silly to me. Even our hot water bottles were queer, big stone jars, and if they fell out of bed they made such a noise. The grand-aunts had their beds warmed up by a big copper thing on a handle called a warming pan!

Uncle Harold was staying at Annagh. I asked him why he didn't go to work like other men, like McConnell. He said, "Child, you have been told before, McConnell is only a thick, a son of the soil. I am a poet and I have to have time to make up the verses." He used say the same thing over and over. It was "they multiplied star upon star." My father said, "Who the hell are 'they?'" and that "Harold Frazer was a damned fool." Aunt Kate said my father's language was awful and my mother said, "They won't take you in the army unless you have bad language." Auntie Mona said that her brother Harold spent his life "going on spongers' sporting tours." I didn't know what they meant and she said "He goes where he doesn't have to pay!" Uncle Harold gave me one of his poems. It's called "The Last Journey."

Whence comes the sound of tramping feet,
Through that old Flemish town,
It is ten hundred fighting men—whose tired
   feet, on cobbles beat,
Men dressed in Khaki brown.

The smoke and dust of battle, sore feet
   and clouded eyes
The sting of whistling bullets, murmur
   of dying sighs.
Those moments last are fleeting past
   the sun shines in the skies.

For these have said their last farewells
   good-bye to world's ambition,
This little heap of mud and clay, where
   paltry men, alive to-day,
Forget that day's attrition.

Yet, why should we remember? To-morrow
   is the same
Destruction, ruin, slaughter the name
   of "Truth" defame,
Until that day draws nearer, when in an
   awful fear, the gold of human character
Will burn and disappear.

I never saw my Uncle Harold again after that holiday. My mother said he lived in a dream world. She looked at me and said, "and so do you. Stay there, it's the better world of the two." The Frazers were not a happy family.

My mother and Aunt Mona were drinking all the time upstairs in their bedrooms. They kept lots of naggins of whiskey hidden. My mother had a big bottle hidden under a statue of the Sacred Heart. It was hollow and the bottle fitted beautifully. Beatrice told Nanny she knew the bottle was there and she said Beatrice said "what better Man to mind it." Nanny said Beatrice was blasphemous. They used throw the empty bottles out of the window of their bedroom. They let me throw some too, I nearly hit McConnell. My mother laughed and thought it very funny because I wanted to know if the trees would turn into bottles.

Mary, the maid with the "want", was growing a huge tummy. I asked Aunt Mona, "Is Mary very greedy, she has such a fat tummy?" Aunt Mona said, "No, darling, Mary has a baby growing in her tummy." I thought a lot about that. I asked Beatrice, "If Mary has a baby in her tummy, who put it there?" Beatrice nearly choked she laughed so much. She said, "That's the X-mark question. I think McConnell put it there," and she kept laughing. McConnell was feeding the pigs. He smelt of pigs himself. I said, "McConnell, did you put the baby in Mary's tummy?" He threw the bucket across the yard and shouted, "Sweet flyin' Jasus and the lot." I told on him. I told Mary and she said "McConnell will go straight to hell where he belongs." There was really so much to think about.

I had heard an awful thing about the four-poster bed. I didn't ever want to sleep in it again. I was in the kitchen and I heard Beatrice telling Mrs West, "They brought Miss Edith (my aunt who drowned herself) up from the river. It was McConnell found her. He carried her up to the house. She was dead and that cold. Mrs Carmody came up from the village to lay her out. We had her lovely in her lace nightgown; in the four-poster bed she was, laying there like a princess, the poor thing."

I flew up to my mother's room. "I'm not going in that four-poster bed any more. I heard Beatrice telling Mrs West that Aunt Edith, when she was dead, was put in that bed." I was frightened and very upset. "Beatrice should keep her trap shut," my mother said.

Aunt Mona and my mother took me into Sligo that afternoon to take my mind off Edith. McConnell drove us in the pony and trap and I was allowed to hold the reins of the pony. His name was Murphy. My mother said it was torture with all the bumps. She said it was like doing Lough Derg sitting down. In Sligo we went into a place with sawdust on the floor and a big brown counter. There were farmers there, with big glasses of dark stuff with foam on top. I asked Auntie Mona, "Where are we?" She said, "We are in a public house." I asked her, "What is a public house?" and she said, "A public house is a place where people go to drink." This was followed by, "Why can't they drink at home?" and my mother said, "They drink at home as well." It was all very confusing.

Aunt Mona said to me, "Why don't you play up to your Aunt Kate?"

"Why?" I said.

"She hates RCs but if you praise the Protestants she might leave you some money in her will." My mother said, "Shut up, Mona." But I thought about this. McConnell drove us back to Annagh. Aunt Kate came out. She said she hoped we were hungry, that there was pig's cheek for dinner. My mother said, "It's easily seen they are only savages." I saw the most awful thing in the kitchen. There was a big black pot

64

on the range with steam coming out of it. Beatrice said, "It's a real treat, do you want a peep? It's your dinner." In the pot was half a pig's face with a snout and an eye. I ran screaming to my mother. She said, "Don't worry, you needn't eat it, just eat the potatoes and vegetables." Such a day. I had heard my drowned aunt was put where I had to sleep and then they cooked a dead pig's face! Anyway I was going to sleep in Aunt Mona's room and Mrs West would be all alone in the four-poster.

At dinner the pig's face was on the table on a big serving dish. My mother kept laughing and saying, "Oh, my God." Aunt Mona asked to be excused. She said afterwards she felt sick! I tried not to look and ate my potatoes and peas. It was hard getting the peas up with a fork. Aunt Kate said, "You may use a spoon for your peas." I answered, "Use a spoon yourself." Uncle Harold was delighted. He said "That's the first time anyone has stood up to that old battle-axe for years." After dinner, I went into the drawing-room. I was going to "play-up" to Aunt Kate to get her money.

I said, "Pardon me."

"What is it, child?" she replied.

I told her "I am learning Protestant prayers."

She looked really pleased. "And why, child, do you like them?"

"No, they are much shorter, that's why." She started looking cross again. My mother said the boys—that's what she called her brothers, my uncles—all of them played up to the grand-aunts so as to be remembered in their will. My father said of the grand-aunts, "Those two damned old women are bigots."

I always felt very sad leaving Annagh, but Uncle

Harold told me, "If you really love a place like this, you can come back any time you like just by thinking of the house, garden and all of us." That was good advice but I couldn't stop the tears coming in my eyes just the same.

9 The Family at Saintbury

It was lovely to see Saintbury again and my black cocker spaniel, Billy. He went crazy with joy. There was one thing I was very worried about. I wondered what my new school my father had chosen for me would be like. Things didn't turn out too badly. He had decided that my sister, Pat, and I would go to a day school in Dun Laoghaire, or, as he always called it, Kingstown. We were happy there and did not kill ourselves working too hard. We caught the eight forty-five train from Killiney station and returned home on the three o' clock. My music was improving all the time. I will never forget the joy of returning home every day, having been so lonely as a boarder in Sion Hill.

I used to cry for hours, especially at night. I'd open my window and look at the moon on the sea over Killiney Bay and cry and cry. From the age of about five until I was twenty-seven, and said good-bye to Saintbury, I cried because I wanted to love both my parents and I could not. I could only choose one of them. When my mother was drunk I hated her. When my father was angry I hated him. I loved him when I saw him on Armistice Day laying a wreath of poppies on the Cenotaph for his regiment, the Connaught Rangers. I loved him when I saw him march past with his old comrades, shoulders back, medals gleaming. I understood his patriotism and pride and saw the proud, handsome younger soldier he once was. My mother I loved for her generosity. She never ever passed a travelling woman with a child without giving her money. A not very pleasant circumstance caused me finally to make my choice and I chose my mother.

I was about twelve years old. One night I was woken by noise and shouting. My father had let my mother in. She was in the hall trying on all fours to crawl to her room. I was shocked, I had never seen her like that before. He was kicking her and calling her a "dirty drunken swine." I did admire what my sister Pat did. She came out of her room brandishing a heavy wooden coat-hanger. She was standing up to her father for the first time and said, "Leave her alone or I'll hit you with this." My father stopped kicking Mother then and Nanny came out of the nursery and she and Essie, the parlour-maid, helped Mother to her room and put her to bed. Doctor Pim, our local GP, was sent for and gave her an injection to put her to sleep through the night. This happened frequently: sometimes total strangers would leave her home, or she would go into one of the cottages in the village and stay there for hours. Usually all her money was gone. No one knew where she had been on these escapades and she always said in the morning that she couldn't remember where she had been! It was probably true because she did suffer from blackouts.

After that particular episode of watching a woman on the ground being kicked by a man, from then on I stood by my mother drunk or sober, come hell or high water. As in religion, I trained myself to love the sinner, not the sin. We had a funny relationship, but I thank God that I was able to bring some happiness into her life. Being an alcoholic is a sickening, guilt-ridden and friendless state.

One great bone of contention between my father and mother was her befuddled interest in Christian Science. My mother would go on and on about Mrs Mary Baker Eddy, the foundress of Christian Science, and she had a bible and various text books but she could not really take in the meaning of it. I always felt it was her protest against Catholicism because she hated the Church's teachings on hell at that time. My father would wrench the books away from her and try and throw them on the fire. Once he threw her glasses in the fire too. I thought that really low of him. One day in the library there was a big fight: she was quietly reading when he tore her Christian Science books from her. She retaliated by calling him a "damned cripple." Sensing trouble, my sisters, Pat, Betty and I left the room. We sat on the top of the stairs, half fascinated, half afraid. My mother screamed "Charles, stop! You're breaking my arm!" "Damn cripple, am I? I've more strength in my left arm than you have in your whole body." We could hear her chair grinding across the room as he twisted her arm. I was so afraid he'd break it but at the same time I knew "damned cripple" was breaking his heart.

I said to my father once—and it took courage—"I am very upset over this terrible fighting." He replied, "It's none of your business." None of my business, except that I was to be treated for endogenous or recurring depression for the rest of my life.

A priest friend of the family, Father Tom Grogan, once said that whatever my mother did, she always rated forgiveness. To me, that was a debatable point! One of the things that always annoyed her during periods of sobriety, was that she felt the Catholic Church had too much money and did not distribute enough of it to "Christ's poor." On this issue, she decided to act. She went into Dublin, up Grafton Street and turned off of it into Clarendon Street where there is a beautiful and well-known Catholic church. She took all the money out of the petition boxes for candles (how she managed it we never knew). With a big bag full of mostly coppers, she traversed the poor parts of the city, flinging handfuls of coins to the poor of the area. She kept enough for two strong whiskeys for herself! She said the money had gone where Christ meant it to go (including the two whiskeys!) and not into the coffers of over-fed prelates! The parish priest contacted my father and if the pun over a quasi-religious issue may be excused, there was hell to pay.

Another, perhaps less funny, incident occurred at Ballybrack Church, Saint Alphonsus and Columba's, near to Saintbury. Confirmation for the children of the parish was taking place. My mother, having returned from Dublin on the Ballybrack bus, went into the church. This she often did, not to pray, but to write down all the things that were getting on her nerves! She told me it was a cold wet day and there was no heating on in the church, which was packed with shivering little girls and boys in their finery. Mother said the bishop was old and doddering and his homily to the children went on and on. She stood up and shouted, "Shut up, these children are frozen. For God's sake, get on with it." She was hustled, unrepentant, from the church.

Another day I got off the bus and took a short cut through the Church Walk and when I emerged at the National School I saw a crowd of yelling children. On closer inspection I realised that they were surrounding a woman. Mother was sitting on the road, back to the wall, drunk out of her skull. She kept dipping into her handbag and flinging money to the children who screamed, "More, more, more." I chased them away. I tried to get her up and couldn't, but luckily a kindly neighbour came to my aid. We got her into his car and to my horror, she was sick in the car. I was only a child and I didn't know what to do.

I will never forget the story of baby Rita. Every week Mother used take a taxi into Dublin to the slums. Then, in the thirties and forties, there were real slums. People in those rat-infested dwellings accepted her, probably because she felt totally in rapport with them. She told me the woman in one dwelling she visited had given birth to her seventh baby, five and a half pounds, born on the floor on a filthy mattress. Her drunken husband only used her for sex and had no use for the other children. Mother asked the woman if the baby had a name and she answered apathetically, "I didn't bother naming her, Mam, this one won't live." My mother named the little baby Rita. She went to see her every day, put her on Bengers food and bought warm baby clothes. She asked Nanny's advice—"Shouldn't the baby have a bath?" Nanny, who was fully trained in the care of infants, told Mother that a baby as premature as Rita was, and as underweight, should only be bathed in warm olive oil.

One day my mother came home mad drunk in a terrible state. She had gone to visit baby Rita as usual, and found the pictures and mirror in the filthy room covered in black crepe, and the little one laid out in a cardboard box. The mother had bathed her baby in olive oil as instructed, but in boiling oil, and the poor little body was covered in blisters. The family and neighbours were reciting the Rosary. Mother told me she screamed at them, "Damn you and your bloody Rosary, you have murdered the baby." Did the mother do it on purpose, could anyone be that stupid? She already had six children that she could not feed. I felt so sorry for Mother; she had lost a baby of her own and I felt she mourned them both in this horrible tragedy. She created a dreadful scene and illogically blamed Nanny. She yelled at her, "*You* told her about the oil, *you* murdered the baby." Poor Nanny was terribly upset.

Killiney was slow to move with the times at the end of the 1920s and the beginning of the 30s. There were two hansom cabs parked at the Ballybrack cross-roads. We lived exactly half-way between Killiney and Ballybrack. My mother, usually inebriated, always took old Dan's cab, one shilling up the hill to Saintbury. It was a steep hill for the poor horses, especially carrying my overweight mother.

My father saw that I was only messing at day school. When I was twelve he asked me how would I like to go to Farnborough. I did not want to go. But that was it—I had to go. Besides, he said my Dublin accent was getting worse and he didn't want me making friends with the children of Sinn Féiners.

10 Farnborough

Farnborough Hill in Hampshire. Some journey for a small girl. My father drove me, in tears, down to Dun Laoghaire to board the mail-boat for Holyhead. I was told to watch out for other girls wearing green coats and red berets. I was a very immature twelve-and-a-half. Luckily, I met some other girls going to Farnborough. They were a bit condescending as they were used to travel. No tears for them. For a child it was quite a journey. At Holyhead the train to Euston and for me the terror of wondering if I would see my school trunk come off the train. Then I asked a porter to get me a taxi to cross London to Waterloo Station and then another train to Aldershot, followed by quite a long bus drive to Farnborough Hill. Farnborough was run by a French order of nuns, the Sisters of Christian Education, and my reception there was quite different from the Irish convent, Sion Hill. There, the girls had teased me at first because I had a sister a film star, but they were soon friendly and the nuns were kind also. Sister Thérèse used kiss us all goodnight (she had a moustache and we dreaded it); however, they were caring. But this was England. No one teased me. I was politely ignored. The nuns were polite disciplinarians. We had to curtsy to Reverend Mother and to the mistress of classes.

Farnborough had been the palace home of the Empress Eugénie, the wife of Napoleon II, who lived there from 1881 until 1920. It was beautiful and impressive, situated on a hill (hence Farnborough Hill) and surrounded by acres of grounds and the most magnificent rhododendrons in every shade from pink to mauve. The palace must have been kept in trust as all the furnishings, drapes and pictures belonged to the 1870s period. The empress had lived there from 1881 to 1920. She, her husband and son are buried in the crypt of a church she built there, Saint Michael's. The nuns lived in the palace and the girls in a built-on ordinary looking building. We had to walk a mile every day to the school, an ugly three-storey house in Farnborough village.

For me, who had so few clothes, the uniform was marvellous: a smartly cut green coat and red beret and a beautiful blazer striped in two shades of green with an ornate crest on the pocket. For every day, a navy tunic bound in green stripes, school tie and fawn shirt blouses. On Sundays we wore what we liked and there was fierce competition. Yet I was unhappy. To me, it was like being in a very civilised prison. All our letters (except to home) incoming and outgoing were read by a nun who looked as if she enjoyed that job. I was so homesick and because I had never bothered to work the nuns said I had an un-used brain. I was backward in every subject, even games, and I feared and hated gym where two masculine-looking women, in very short tunics, with muscular legs and arms, forced us to do somersaults over a wooden horse. They never smiled. Far worse was the swimming pool for those of us who where afraid of the water. We had to stand around the pool at the ready and when the teacher blew the whistle it was obligatory to dive in head first. I was always terrified.

As a child I didn't know what caused me to be so sad and unhappy. The grown-ups said I was moody but it was not so. Later in life, the psychiatrist I went to explained that children of an alcoholic parent are prone to depression and, of course, I was also a victim of an unstable loveless childhood. I hated those nuns. I was told, whether it was true or not, that their coldness to me was due to the fact that most of them did not like the Irish. I must have presented a problem to them because in the middle of my first term my father, who was in London attending one of his regimental dinners, came down to Farnborough to see me. He and I were entertained to afternoon tea by Reverend Mother in the palace drawing-room. It was very beautiful and I could not take my eyes off the lovely chandeliers. The furniture was a little uncomfortable. Chairs of the 1870s suited the long gowns the ladies wore then. My father said Reverend Mother was "a decent woman." Coming from him that was quite a compliment. After he left, I was placed in a class lower than my age group and this did not help me. All the time I knew that if I wanted to I could do as well as everyone else. But I did not care. I wanted to go back to Saintbury.

Finally, the Easter holidays came and a month at home. Everything there was the same: Nanny fussing around the nursery and Pat and Betty looking far too adult to be in a nursery. My dog Billy was waiting for me. My mother was waiting for me too. She was a little drunk so that was something. I felt, as always, that the house was glad I was back. I soon got back into my routine, wandering round the house and gardens, taking my dog for walks over Killiney Hill, from where that beautiful uncluttered bay outshines, totally, the clutter that is the Bay of Naples. Too soon it was time to go back to Farnborough. My father was very ill. He had pneumonia and I was afraid he might die. He had two nurses, a day and a night nurse. I asked my mother, "Will he die?" She said, "We have to wait for the crisis." There were no antibiotics then and it was a painful, long drawn-out illness. The crisis was actually a two to three-day period where the patient fought for his life and sometimes lost the fight and died. My father also had pleurisy. The constant pain of his war wound had left him a delicate man.

Under all this stress I had to go back to Farnborough. This was the long summer term. In England we did not get our summer holidays until the end of July and we returned at the end of September. In Ireland it was the beginning of June until the first week of September. The English way meant we were missing out the best part of the summer. One of the big traditional occasions at Farnborough, was towards the end of the summer term, when *Hiawatha* was acted in the school grounds. It was very beautiful and the trees and shrubs and the river made it all seem so believable. The school orchestra provided the lovely music from *Hiawatha* and the strongest and most boyish-looking of the senior girls were chosen for the lead. Parents came all very dressed up and the nuns gushed over any titled families, of which there were quite a few. We had strawberries and cream and the palace was open for viewing. Most of the girls were to be debutantes and eventually would be presented at

Court. It was a school for imperialists, rich girls with names like Hathaway-Jones and Pennington-Whitbotham.

My brother Jackie, who was stationed at nearby Aldershot, would come to any soirees and bring me masses of sweets. His army friend, Freddie, said he was so sorry for me being locked up with the nuns that he felt he would like to buy me a car.

I tried to pull up my studies by writing lovely dramatic (and true) essays. One was about when I was five and Count John McCormack was a dinner guest at Saintbury. He sat me on his knee and the moon was shining over Killiney Bay and for me he sang "The Little Boy Blue." There were tears in everyone's eyes as that beautiful voice soared over the bay. Then he said, "Now little one, you sing for me." Too ready I was! I ran over to the piano and with one finger banged out a very rude (I didn't know it was rude) song about a bonny Scotsman and the wind blowing up his petticoat. My father was furious. I was sent to bed. Mother Josephine, our English teacher, was furious too because I had written the full verse in the essay, leaving nothing to her chaste imagination. That was another black mark. Here began a build up of trouble I inadvertently created, not having the good sense to play it the nuns' way.

Then there was a row over the photographs in our sleeping quarters. We slept six to a dormitory. There was a shelf beside each bed for our bits and pieces. I put up three lovely glossies of my sister Maureen and Johnny Weissmuller as Tarzan and Jane, one with her leaning against his manly chest, both gazing over the lake, another with Chita, the chimp, and one of Maureen in her "piece of a dress," posed with one foot dangling in the water. They were taken down by one of the nuns. I put them back. This went on. Finally, a summons to the sanctum sanctorum, Reverend Mother's office. "Take your hands out of your pockets. These photographs are not suitable for a convent." Instead of holding my whist, I said, "There is nothing wrong with them, I am proud of my sister. My mother says to the pure all things are pure." The Reverend Mother was white with anger; the photos were confiscated. The following week I was summoned to Reverend Mother again. My latest composition was on her desk. This was entitled "My sister told me." She had told me and the story was true but not fit for a convent.

The essay was about nannies. It began, "I, myself, was very unhappy with Nanny, really because she did not care about me and she took such a pride in my younger sisters Pat and Betty." My sister Maureen told me that she and our brother Jackie had a much worse time than I did. It was a horror story. The year was 1917. Maureen was seven and Jackie five. Nannies started to take over their lives. They were imported from England. The family was living in our grandparent Frazers' house, Riversdale, Co Roscommon. Father had a horror of Irish brogues and did not want any of his children to grow up with them. The children were to be absolutely British. The nannies were all young and charmed father into thinking that they really cared for their charges, whereas their cruelty was unbelievable. One cold night when Maureen had done something naughty, Nanny put her in a cold bath, holding her under the water until she turned blue from the cold and was in such a state of shock that she could not even cry. One nanny outlasted all the others. Her name was Doreen Ranger and from looking at old snapshots I could see she was a pretty girl in her early twenties. It appears my father thought a lot of her and her apparent devotion to Jackie, his only son. Maureen said it was hard to convince father that she was other than she looked. She made that seven year old girl steal for her—small items from father's desk, expensive writing paper, pens, stamps—blaming Maureen to her father as a thief. Maureen says she does not remember one kind word from her. The worst was to come when five-year old Jackie soiled his pants. Holding him over her knees, Doreen Ranger forced the horrible brown stuff down his throat while he vomited and choked. In spite of her dire threats, Maureen went crying and hysterical to her father. Nanny Ranger described Maureen as not only a liar but psychopathic. But between them, the children convinced father and he fired her. Maureen was amazed that before she left, Nanny Ranger gave her a beautiful doll. She said she took the doll to her room and took its eyes out, then she took it to the end of the garden where the waves lapped at the rocks at high tide. She held the doll under the water until she was so waterlogged that she could not float and watched happily as a wave carried her out to sea. Maureen said she then was about eight but that Nanny had damaged her to an extent from which she could not recover. Day in and day out, she was told "You're ugly, everyone hates you." Because she was only a child, Maureen never thought Nanny could be wrong.

Reverend Mother and Mother Josephine said that they had never read such gross exaggeration in their lives. And even if it were true, one should never wash one's dirty linen in public. They suggested I needed psychiatric attention, that I could be a pathological liar. How I wished that Maureen was not millions of miles away in America. My brother had gone to serve in Palestine at the time of the Arab-Jewish war and my father was too ill. I felt so very unhappy and I had no one to back me up.

Then, there was the matter of the school meals. We sat eight girls to a table with a nun at the head; she served out our helpings of food. We had Mother Fox. I hated her in her waxen bonnet covered with a black veil. The nuns at Farnborough had nasty little black bows under the chin and black ankle-length habits, not long and trailing like the Irish nuns. Spam was the one thing I couldn't eat. One day we had spam. I picked at it in dismay. "Eat your spam, Sheila O'Sullivan," said Mother Fox, because the others had finished. "Here, quick," the girl opposite me said, and proceeded to pile the other seven plates on top of mine. The maid came to take them. "Remove all those plates and give Sheila hers; she will stay here until it's eaten." I thought of Nanny years ago forcing me to eat marrow. I stayed looking at the spam for an hour in the empty refectory until Mother Fox came back.

"All right. For one week you sit at the punishment table." This typical nuns' punishment was a solitary table on a raised rostrum in the middle of the refectory where the offender sat to eat alone. The utter sadism of it.

Only one thing was good: my music was improving all the time, both in technique and depth of feeling. The nuns said of my pianoforte, "At this she is a genius."

I had always had strong telepathic and extra sensory perception skills, and I "knew" that my father was near to death, not just ill but near to death. I wrote long miserable letters to my mother, I never wrote to Pat and Betty because there was never any rapport between us. I even wrote to Nanny, who had got to like me better as I got older. The nuns at Farnborough decided I was a misfit, that I needed psychiatric attention, that I should leave the school. This was because they intercepted one of my letters telling my mother that I had no love or affection shown to me, that I was not allowed to mix with my own age group, but was put with the tiny ones because I was so backward. I was made to feel inadequate and guilty but for what? The nuns made me sleep the night in the infirmary. Someone would pack my clothes. Matron gave me some sedation. I was expelled. I cried myself to sleep. What a reflection it is on those women that I, a thirteen-year-old child, would, if I'd had the means at my disposal, have taken my life in my abject fear and desperation.

The next day my aunts (my father's sisters) dear kind Aunt Maud and Aunt Ned (Edith) drove down from London to fetch me. My cousin Dermot, Aunt Maud's son, cheered me up , just by his good nature and humorous presence. None of them ever rebuked me; they understood my low spirits. I did not even shake hands with the nun who saw us off. She, Sister Preston (they did not take saints' names, like Irish nuns do, but kept their surnames!), was a second-class citizen in the convent as she was in charge of the fitting room for uniforms. She nodded and said, "Well, good afternoon" to my relations. I looked through the back window of the car at the magnificent building and at the colour of the rhododendrons. It was a beautiful place. I wondered if I would ever in my life be as unhappy as this again.

11 Between Schools

At home in Ireland my father was slowly recovering from his illness, but he was certainly not fit enough to deal with me. My Aunt Maud told me I was not going home for three months, but I was to stay with her in her lovely house in London, on Hampstead Heath. My aunts Maud and Ned never in any way chastised me. The time I spent with them, specially Aunt Maud, was what I had always dreamed of. It was exactly like I imagined having a mother who had time for me.

My aunts took me about London with them. We visited glamorous Bond Street, the empire of fashion, Madame Tussaud's Waxworks and the ghoulish Chamber of Horrors where the most heinous of murderers astonished me, because they looked like ordinary people. I spent a lot of time up on Hampstead Heath with my Aunt Maud's dog Rover, a black and white cocker. There the children, and their daddies flew the most wonderful kites and sailed every kind of model craft on the pond. We went to the local Odeon to see my sister in *Tarzan of the Apes*. The year was 1935. I looked at my beautiful sister and wished I knew her. It was funny to have a sister and not know her. I thought how beautiful she was and what an uninteresting girl I was.

My Aunt Maud took me to a hairdresser's and bought me new clothes and for the first time in my life I felt a little more self confident. My cousin Dermot, who would then have been almost twenty-three, was always changing jobs, and drank a fair amount. His drinking did not upset me. I thought he was very funny. It did not affect my life though no doubt his mother worried. He was always nice to me, and I was not going to get involved in their family worries, I had enough to face when I went back to Ireland. My Aunt Maud said she thought that the trouble at Farnborough was due to the fact that I had a lot of my mother in me. She said to me, "There is a lot of good in you, and a lot of your mother too." That annoyed me. The Frazers looked down on the O'Sullivans as common and dull. Common they were not, dull they were! Even at fourteen I could see that they had none of the sparkle or good looks of the Frazers. They were narrow in their strict Catholicism and bad-minded enough to believe my mother was having an affair with a priest, Father Tom Grogan. She did not have a sexual alliance, just a stupid crush. But it was hot gossip among the O'Sullivan relations, and the consensus in Cork was that she was having an affair.

I never really knew my father's eldest sister, Florence, who lived in Cork. All I know is that the lady was strict and a paragon of virtues. My mother's drinking and what the Cork relations decided was her affair with a priest provided interesting gossip and was fed into the communal pool by my nice little Aunt Ned who used to stay for long holidays in Saintbury, really an observation tour of the behaviour of my Mother and indeed of us all. When they referred to my father, they said, "Poor Charles is a martyr."

However that time in London was made a nice time. My Aunt Ned insisted on taking me to confession, she said to a "very nice priest." I found it a very difficult confession because having initially, as all penitents do, said "Bless me Father for I have sinned" I did not really think I had sinned. I thought the nuns had sinned! The priest, I thought, agreed with me, because he kept saying "You're still only a child, God love you." I did not look nearly fourteen.

Finally I went home, back to Ireland and Saintbury. My father met me at the mail boat, looking ill and fragile. He was icy cold to me. My mother was in the car, drunk as a coot, but at least she was pleased to see me and my dog Billy was ecstatic with joy. Nothing had changed. Nanny was still dutifully minding my sisters Pat and Betty. Pat was fourteen, Betty eleven. They were attending day school. They didn't know it then, but my father had put their names down for a convent boarding school, Mount Anville, Dundrum, in Dublin. The nuns were the Order of the Sacred Heart, très snob. Pat was due to go the following September, but Betty had a few years reprieve.

Saintbury seemed neglected and my father spent almost every day at his club, seldom returning for dinner. This was the Royal Irish Yacht Club in Dun Laoghaire of which he was Rear-Commodore. He owned a beautiful motor launch yacht, Ikona. But she did roll a lot and the smell of paraffin from the engine made me feel sick, especially when Tommy, the paid hand, would pop up from the galley offering thick fresh bread covered in greengage jam. Father took the helm with his left hand; he wore a white yachting cap

*From left: Mona Frazer, Chinese Amah and
Mary Eva Frazer at Riversdale, Co Roscommon*

*The author's grand-aunts, Kate and Anna
Frazer*

Edith Frazer who took her life,
aged twenty-four

Mary Eva Frazer, the author's
mother, on her wedding day

Charles O'Sullivan, father of the author

From left: Jack, Sheila and Maureen O'Sullivan in 1923

The author, Sheila O'Sullivan, in Bournemouth, aged five

The author at the age of twenty-four

and seemed happy. He spent most of his days with friends of his own vintage, retired professional and army men. Women were taboo and a red rope across the balcony separated the sexes. Friday night was ladies' night and Father dined at home, "I can't bear the noise of those damned women screaming," he would say.

The house was quiet and lonely as my mother was out every day too. She went to Dublin every day, except Sunday. She lunched at the Hibernian Hotel in Dawson Street and spent the rest of the day drinking in the Hibernian Buttery. Twice a week she dined with a fast priest, who was just known as Guinness (for obvious reasons). He was sponging drinks and free meals; she was lonely and needed company.

Mother had this amazing panache. I recall one occasion when she was standing me lunch in the Hibernian Hotel. The head waiter was intimidating, to say the least. When we entered the dining room Mother said, "A table for two, please." He replied, "I must ask madam to wait half an hour as all the tables are taken." My mother pointed to a space and said, "In that event you can put a table there," and he did. I do not want to sound egotistic, as if I was the only one who suffered trauma because of my mother's drinking. I am sure that my sisters Pat and Betty suffered equally, but at least they had a mother figure in Nanny. She loved them, and the shelter of the nursery was theirs.

We had a lot of ex-service men calling at the house. It took Father about three minutes to find out if they really were "ex-service." He used bark out "What regiment, battalion, when, where, rank, number?" The poor chaps really did earn their two and sixpence! Even I got to know if they were for real or not, by the cut of their gib my father would say. Our family had quite a long of hangers on. I was too naive to realise this. My mother was hospitable and the six-thirty callers were always invited to seven-thirty dinner, plus the charade of the Major and his lady at table. Once an honourable son of a Lord came to dinner. My mother liked that, but the food that night was awful, and my father had no teeth in, they'd gone to the dental mechanic to be trimmed off. My mother kept saying, "this is awful," and exploding with laughter as the poor man sucked in his soup.

Father had a beautiful Siamese cat called Tim. For some reason he only ever spoke German to the cat. Tim loved him, and him alone; he would arch his back and spit at all the rest of us! We had a family cat called Nicky, short for Nicodemus. She was always wild and if someone touched her new born kittens she ate them. We had three dogs, all black cockers and all called Tony so we never felt sad if the dog died. They were all over-fed and full of fleas. Father also had a German roller-canary, Jim. Jim's cage was on a pulley and he was hoisted up to the ceiling in case Tim, the cat, decided to have a go at him. He sang so beautifully but my mother fed him bread, he blew up like a tennis ball and finally died.

All in all, I missed about one year of schooling. I don't think my father knew where to send me. By now I was nearly fifteen. Finally Father sent for me and told me I was going to the Convent of the Assumption in London, 23 Kensington Square.

12

23, Kensington Square

My Aunt Minnie, my father's sister, had been a nun in the Assumption Convent at 23, Kensington Square. Apparently she died in her forties. No one said what she died of, and my Father was quite uninterested in her. "A poor specimen with bad eyesight," was all he ever called her. My father and mother had been married in the convent chapel. How I dreaded it—more English nuns.

It never mattered how rough or cold the weather was; my Father made me go. I remember crossing on the boat called the *Princess Maud*. She was badly stabilised and I dreaded the journey. However I was becoming a little more self-confident. On the train from Holyhead to Euston, I would go into the dining car, order my meal and afterwards tip the waiter, whereas formerly, when I was en-route for Farnborough, aged twelve and a half, it was a bun eaten in the lavatory. I used to take a taxi from Euston to Kensington. I had my own little room there, or cell, as it was called. It was lovely because I looked straight down on Kensington Gardens and Frampton's famous statue of Peter Pan. I used to dream that one day I would have children and that I would call the boy Peter and the girl Wendy.

The convent and adjoining chapel stood on four acres of ground in the heart of London, which were divided up into tennis courts, netball courts and well kept gardens. The nuns were kind and their habits looked like Dior gowns: purple with a heavy white cord around the waist and white veils. On special days they wore beautiful long white cloaks. The teaching was good and it was here that I developed my love of writing and reading.

Kensington Convent had none of the glamour of Farnborough. In fact it was quite a shabby old place. It looked as if time had stood still and the place had never been done up. The parlour, or reception room, was panelled, as were the corridors. The refectory and class rooms had well-worn desks and tables with names and dates engraved by former pupils. Most of the school was distempered in mustard. Those of us who had a private room, or cell, were allowed to decorate them as we wished. The tennis and netball courts were hard courts, but on the whole the place had a shabby gentility about it and a homely warmth that was so lacking at Farnborough. The Assumption nuns were especially kind to those of us who were boarders and suffered from homesickness like me. The Matron, Nurse Doherty was Irish, as was our maths teacher, Miss O'Connor. They both spoiled me and I was of course delighted.

I was growing up and I had got fat, all five foot of me. Most of the fat was deposited on my bosom and in convents, one is not allowed to have bosoms. Then I plucked out all my eyebrows, to be in fashion. In the thirties all the girls had those arched eyebrows. The first time I did it there was panic because I could not find an eyebrow pencil. I had to use a greasy black crayon. The nuns nearly had a fit when they saw me. I looked like a little fat top-heavy bug! To make things harder, all through my school days I was known as "Maureen O'Sullivan's sister." This was my only claim to fame and I hated the notoriety.

I made no effort at my studies, except for English and music, but I always had a starring role in school plays. No one cared about my progress so I never tried. My father seemed to have lost hope where I was concerned, and hence it appeared to me that he had lost all interest in my studies. My mother never showed any interest so she did not count. I became so fat and lethargic that the school doctor decided I was low in thyroid and pituitary, the glands that control growth and memory retention, and he put me on the appropriate tablets.

I wrote and told my Father. He was furious because his own GP told him this was "dangerous" treatment and highly specialised. My Aunt Maud took me to her doctor for a second opinion. He said I was a typical case of environmental disturbance because of my home life, my mother's drinking and all the rows and tensions. This Doctor Parsons was a kindly man and the first to make the diagnosis that I was suffering from depression which often affects children of an alcoholic parent. I was given tablets but they did not work. I was to find out that I had something I would have to learn to live with.

My very first day in Kensington Convent I felt unwell. The kind old lay sister (lay sisters did the housework and cleaning) Sister Abyssia put me to bed. I was fifteen and I had got my first period. I had never had any sex instruction and I was very frightened. I had everything muddled. I worried and worried and everyone noticed how ill I looked. Because I had had no sex education I was convinced that I was going to have a baby.

Reverend Mother wrote home to my father. He must have told the nuns about my mother and her problem, because they never referred to her. I don't know what my father wrote in reply, but I was summoned to Reverend Mother's sanctum sanctorum. "Sheila dear, you are not pregnant," she said. My father's letter was on her desk—he wrote with his left hand in back-slanting writing. She went on, "Matron will tell you all you need to know and your friends will be told." She actually smiled. "Go now dear and stop worrying. Go into the chapel and sit there quietly and listen to what Jesus will say to you." I curtsied, "Thank you Mother." I felt disappointed! I ran to the empty chapel, I looked at the little red lamp on the altar telling us He was present and I sat and waited for Jesus to talk to me. He said nothing, so after ten minutes I got fed up and went to join my friends.

My pianoforte improved by leaps and bounds, I had an Austrian lady, Madame Fia Fastré, who would alternate between raging at me, and then crying because she would say, "mein Gott, this one's a genius." She wanted only Grieg and Chopin all the time and I got fed up because I wanted Bach and Beethoven. That music was wonderful to me, because I felt I could express all my anger, my joy, and my love of God through that medium.

Naturally I was interested in boys and then I had a fellow at home who was at least fifteen years older than me. He was a rugby international but for my part it was only a school girl crush. But he did write to me care of my aunt in Hampstead. The nuns opened all our outgoing and incoming mail, and boy friends were taboo! Mother St Ignace (sneaky boots!) used sit for hours devouring our letters. My fellow's name was Frank and I got frightened of him, because I didn't want him to be serious. He said he'd wait for me but I didn't want anyone waiting for me. I got quite panicky and dodged him when I went home. I was always afraid of affection, because I had never really known it.

In 1936 Maureen, now a big star and married to Australian-born director and producer John Farrow, was coming to England to make a film with the then leading heart-throb Robert Taylor. The Film *A Yank at Oxford* is the story of a brash young Yank's initiation into Oxford University. Maureen and Robert Taylor and indeed John Farrow were all young, beautiful, rich and famous. The school was agog about Robert Taylor. I became important overnight with everyone begging "Please get me his autograph and Maureen's too." I was in for a taste of high living. The boarders were allowed weekends out with suitable relations from Saturday at noon till Sunday at nine pm. I was to stay at the Dorchester on Saturday night with my famous sister. I was then sixteen and, thank heaven, much slimmer. The big day arrived and a chauffeur-driven limo called for me at twelve sharp, to escort me to the Dorchester. Maureen, then twenty-six, was waiting for me in the foyer. She looked beautiful in black with a huge pink hat. I felt shy and gauche. However my French was good enough for me to understand the long luncheon menu and even order my meal in French. It was gradually dawning on me that a good education is a very worthwhile asset. Soon I lost my shyness and the day sped by just talking and laughing with that sister I have always loved, Maureen.

John Farrow was not due for another week so Maureen was taking Aunt Edith and me to dinner at the Hungaria and then to the theatre. I was a little worried about my long pink dress. I thought it childish, but Maureen said it was right for a sixteen year old. She dressed my long hair with lilies of the valley and loaned me a long, beautifully cut, black velvet coat to wear over the dress. I loved the gypsy music at the Hungaria and we had a box at the theatre for Noel Coward's musical, *Crest of the Wave*. Strangely I felt religious at the theatre, I think I felt happy and it was so wonderful because I had never felt totally right before, and even though it ended it was wonderful.

During the school week I had a surprise visit from Geve's the West-End tailors. Two gentlemen came to fit me for riding jacket, jodhpurs and boots! Needless to say one of the nuns was present to chaperone me! Maureen and John intended taking me riding with them in Rotten Row. I wondered if Robert Taylor might join us. The riding excursion never took place because when filming began the schedule was just too tightly packed. The following weekend Maureen got special permission for me to leave the convent from Friday night till Sunday at nine o'clock. They were starting to shoot the film at Denham Film studios in Oxford and I was to travel down to Denham with Maureen. She had rented a beautiful old English cottage, which had once been the home of philosopher John Locke. It was held in trust so that everything was exactly the same as when Locke had lived there. All his things, his writing paper, pen, books were about and so was he, Maureen and I decided! Neither of us slept a wink. It was an oakbeam cottage and in the nature of old houses it had a "night" language of its own; everything creaked. At sixteen I was, as I have always been, very conscious of the paranormal.

The next day, a lovely sunny one, they were shooting a scene with Maureen and Robert Taylor having a cuddle on top of a haystack. I was quite amazed to hear Taylor say to my sister, "Quit picking your nose, Maureen." Not at all romantic. He gave me a photograph of himself which made me the envy of the whole school. It was signed, "To Sheila from your good friend Bob Taylor." I used to put it and one of Maureen as Jane with Johnny Weissmuller as Tarzan, he of the wide manly chest, on my dressing table. Mother Margaret would remove Tarzan and Jane and put them in the drawer. Not suitable for a convent. Bob Taylor told me, "I have a little Irish girl friend back in California." Maureen said he was referring to Barbara Stanwyck, who was Irish.

A Yank at Oxford was a simple story about a brash young man, Taylor, who is sent to Oxford. He falls in love with the Dean's daughter, Maureen. At first everyone thoroughly dislikes him for his overbearing attitudes. Eventually by excelling at sports, he becomes what the British call "a good chap" and wins the admiration of his colleagues and the heart of his girlfriend.

Maureen went back to America, and I had a change of heart, I decided not to be a nun! It was only a rather romantic dream a lot of girls go through. To prove that I was not stupid I started to actually work and even I was amazed at the results. I was just as intelligent as every one else. I won my "aspirant's" ribbon, purple and white with a medal. This was given to those who aspire to higher things and finally, one could get a

"Child of Mary" ribbon, only by being a real goody goody. One was then a prefect, a nuns' pet! I never got that one. But my music was getting better and better and I worked really hard. My first ever good school report was sent home. I was so excited. My mother wouldn't really be interested but I knew my father would.

I never heard a word about it. No one cared, and something in me died, and I never worked hard at anything again. I messed about with my music, playing boogie woogie and popular rubbish. I was supposed to stay in the Convent until I was eighteen, but I nagged at my father to let me leave at seventeen. Knowing I was only messing in that expensive school, my Father gave in. The nuns were very upset. I had told them I was going to be a film star, which they thought meant very dangerous living and they wanted me to come back as a parlour boarder and study Montessori teaching. Parlour boarders were young ladies and students who lived in a separate part of the convent, but were free to come and go as they wished. Mother Imelda said, "You are so good with the little ones and you could use your acting ability with them." I think the nuns knew what my problems at home were, and in their kindly way were trying to keep me under their wing. I wanted to go home. I loved Saintbury, and at the back of it all, though it was a strange kind of loving, I loved my father and mother. I felt that what ever she did, mother would have someone who understood her if I was there because I could accept her exactly as she was. We were not a demonstrative family: I never kissed my father or my mother, and certainly not my brother or sisters.

So I left the convent, in tears I must admit. Madame

Fastré, my music teacher, wept. She said, "she is a genius, a true genius." The matron, Nurse Doherty, cried. I promised to go back and visit them.

13

An End to Schooling

There I was home, the finished product of a British education, with an English accent, and a lot of confused ideas, especially the desire to become a film star with the minimum effort. I hadn't much to recommend me, or so I thought.

We were coming up to the time when gracious living was on the way out and it was getting to be very hard to find servants. We got some real hopeless cases and my mother had to show them "how to wait table," whereas in previous years they had arrived for duty properly trained. I remember one very select dinner party when Gertie, the new parlourmaid, handed the potatoes around in the saucepan they were cooked in. Neither Father or Mother batted an eyelid; they acted as if it were an everyday occurrence.

At fifty-eight, father seemed an old man to me. Mother was then aged forty-eight and she weighed fourteen stone, nearly twice her normal weight, although she still had a beautiful face. She was bloated with drink and starting into the menopause.

Anyone who has lived with an alcoholic will know how obnoxious they can get, dirty, reeking of sick and booze and always telling lies, lies. Things got really tough when my Mother fell madly in love with the local curate. He was a colourful character, fat, easy going, quite a talented artist and an accomplished pianist who ran the local swing band. He was known as Father Kerry (because of his accent). In my opinion he was a bastard. For years he accepted weekly pocket money and presents galore from Mother, among them a piano and a most handsome piano accordion, but when she got too troublesome he would report her to my father. In all fairness she gave him a very hard time. I have less respect for the collar than the man who is wearing it. I am not and never will be anti-clerical. There is the rotten apple in every barrel and Father Kerry was one.

One night when Mother was returning from Dublin, with a lot of drink taken, she decided to call at the presbytery. It was ten thirty and the housekeeper, who was in her dressing gown, refused to let her in. My mother pushed her aside and virtually broke in. She went straight upstairs and into Father Kerry's bedroom. He was, she told me, in the situation of one leg in and one out of his black trousers. Of course when he saw her he was nearly apoplectic. In flew the other priest, a dry austere man. He said, "I have never hit a woman before," and caught Mother a clip on the jaw that knocked her out. He was protecting his fat friend's virginity—or so he thought! My mother hated sex, so his virginity was quite safe. She was suffering from a drunken obsessional neurosis. That reverend father packed some punch. I have never seen a more colourful black eye than my mother's.

After that episode Father Kerry was moved to an

adjacent parish. This was ridiculous since it was within walking distance of our home and my mother was off to Mass at the crack of dawn to gaze at the portly vision of her dearly loved priest. She presented him with a magnificent monstrance for the church. The monstrance is used for exposition of the Blessed Sacrament. Mother said that whenever this was elevated at the ceremony of Benediction, she imagined that she saw his face in it—some blasphemy!

John Charles Mc Quaid was installed as Archbishop of the diocese of Dublin. He was a scholarly austere man and, as far as matters appertaining to the Catholic Church were concerned, he was unbendable. Obviously the rather silly story of mother's infatuation with the portly curate came to His Grace's ears and he took action. The village of Ballybrack mourned his leaving, the end of the swing band, and our teenage visits to the always open presbytery for tea and a sing-song. Father Kerry did have his good points, in those stringent days. As a priest he was before his time. The AB, as Father Kerry always referred to him, had him posted to the heart of the country and that passion soon faded from my mother's heart.

Socially I was in demand because of my party piece, the piano accordion. As a child I had started out with a melodeon and then graduated to the accordion. I was good but because I had no singing voice, I felt self-conscious. I didn't know what to do with my face and was too shy to mime a song. Parties for the young in their homes were called "hops" and those of us who could, took it in turn to play the piano. I remember one fellow who had his twenty-first party in Stanley's Café on Killiney beach. I wondered why I'd been invited as they were Protestants and in

Killiney in the 1930s Protestants and Catholics did not socialise. I was soon to find out. I played that piano, a bad piano, from nine till two in the morning and my reward was, "three cheers for Sheila O'Sullivan!" So much for ecumenism! By this time my classical music was ruined and I was playing what Father called "rubbish" popular music.

At Saintbury we did have some wonderful parties, not "hops" but *de rigueur*. The drawing room with its beautiful parquet floor and bay windows over-looking Killiney Bay was perfect. We usually had a hundred guests. My Mother would rig up little corners with a screen or large plant sheltering a chaise longue, over which she hung "for sitting out" notices. I used love doing the flowers and since it was such a big house the floral displays had to be done on a very large scale. There were four greenhouses to supply flowers.

Apart from the dances, which were of course evening dress and black tie, we had *thé dansants* on the first Sunday of every month, from four till six o'clock. A man playing a violin and a lady pianist were hired. A sumptuous tea was served in the large dining room and guests wandered from the tea to the dance floor. The music was fox trots, waltzes, the Lambeth walk which was just in, and tunes like "If you hadn't asked me to dance," "Blue Moon," "September in the Rain." Dress was important: men naturally wore collar and tie and suits, the ladies pretty beaded afternoon frocks. People met plenty of people and these parties were very popular. No one minded if Mother was too drunk; they were just having a good time at our expense. Normally, after these Sunday afternoons a chosen few remained and there was always someone among us who could play the piano, plus my own pièce de resistance, my piano accordion.

I was fairly adept at drawing and painting and my father was very proud of the Christmas cards I designed (to his order) for various friends of his at the Royal St George Yacht Club. Caricatures were the speciality of my Mother and me and we used laugh ourselves silly over them. However a number of people took offence. "Ridicule," they said, so I gave it up.

14 Lough Derg

Mother called herself a Christian Scientist, though she could never accept their basic "mind over matter" belief and philosophies like "sickness and illness are all in the mind." She said she hated Catholicism for two reasons: the Church's teaching that those who died in mortal sin went to hell to burn for all eternity, and the fact she could not sever the chains that tied her to the Church.

A strange paradox was the number of times she "did" the Lough Derg Pilgrimage. I think she felt a certain amount of guilt for all the trouble she was giving and the pilgrimage offered a masochistic purging. The two of us decided to go on the pilgrimage. Lough Derg in Co Donegal is known as St Patrick's Purgatory. Allegedly St Patrick stayed on the island on the lake and fasted and did penance. All sorts of people go there for the same reasons: to do penance for sin and to cleanse themselves of guilt by three days and nights of torture. I was very young when I went on the pilgrimage (not quite seventeen).

It rained all the time and it was bitterly cold. I'm told it is always cold and more often than not raining.

In a way I was quite frightened that I had committed myself to the pilgrimage, especially as every time I questioned my mother, she said "It's torture, it's torture." So I have to admit I only went on the Lough Derg pilgrimage because at seventeen I was sanguine enough to believe that four days in St Patrick's Purgatory would whittle down my figure and the good Lord would hand over the unobtainable fellow I was after. Two days before we left, I looked out of the window and saw Mother, hobbling barefoot over the gravelled drive. She was practising for Lough Derg. Obeying the rule of fasting, we fasted from midnight on Thursday and on a very cold Friday morning were up early and away. The train journey was hell. It was June but everyone was bundled up; heavy Arans, oilskins and scarves. During the train journey, the Rosary was recited over and over again, relieved by a break for hot or cold water and hard rye bread; salt and pepper were sprinkled into the hot water to make "Lough Derg Soup."

After the train journey to Letterkenny, we (the lost tribe of Israel) boarded the waiting buses and when we arrived at the lake we had to walk across a soggy field. It was windy and bitterly cold. The lake was choppy, the island bleak and the row-boats over-crowded; rain lashed down and desperate attempts were made to put up umbrellas. The pilgrims were singing "Star of the Sea," when we felt a hell of a bump; our boat had hit the rocks! A woman screamed, "We'll all be drowned." A fat priest stood up, making the boat rock violently, "Start the Rosary," he shouted. This was too much for my mother. She called "Sit down and shut up! To hell with the Rosary! Put down the umbrellas and get us off the rocks." It was good advice and we felt the boat get afloat again.

At the jetty everyone handed in their shoes for a pink ticket. It was the last we were to see of them for four days. We stepped barefooted onto the island through cold muddy puddles and left our bags in the dormitory where we were to sleep our one night's sleep of the pilgrimage. The penance began immediately.

The stations of the cross were circles of sharp stones and rocks under which relics were buried. In the middle of each circle was a cross. The order of devotion was to go thirteen times around each circle, reciting the Rosary non-stop. In the middle of each recitation one had to kneel for the words, "We adore thee O Christ." It was nearly impossible to kneel on the stones and very painful. I was slow, but my Mother flew round with the speed and agility of a mountain goat.

For one of the stations one had to stand against the church wall, arms akimbo against a large cross and, swinging out the arms, call out three times (feeling an awful ejit) "I renounce Satan, and all his works and pomps." When my mother's turn came, she had forgotten that her umbrella was slung around her wrist and she caught a sour-faced nun a crack on the nose! Another station was situated at the water's edge and we knelt in the cold water there. So on we went, stumbling around and around the stations. I looked down at my feet; they were blue from the cold and my big toe was bleeding. I felt nothing, just strangely detached. In my ears the repetitious drone, "Holy Mary Mother of God," went on and on. My mother kept repeating, "It's torture," with masochistic glee.

It was interesting to observe the other pilgrims.

They ranged from young to very old and were from every walk of life. We were all stripped of our dignity; being fully dressed yet bare-footed not only humbled us, but made us look ridiculous. But the pilgrims never faltered. If anyone stumbled or fainted, someone would stop and help. Except for our breaks for food, tea, hot water and rye bread, we did not converse. When we did talk, nearly everyone shared their reasons for coming, some were doing the pilgrimage for a relative who was terminally ill, or indeed for their own illness, others with marital problems, but fifty percent were there for one reason, to do penance!

I found the devotion and piety of the pilgrims touchingly impressive. It made me realise more than ever how Irish Catholics, myself included, value their faith. Although one could have a laugh and although I was with Mother, who invariably saw the amusing side of everything, this still did not alter the fact that though I was fat and lovelorn, something touched my heart at Lough Derg.

That first day was hard and I felt so hungry. We were allowed smoke during tea breaks but any hidden snacks (there were very few) were taken away by the Legion of Mary stewards. And the worst was yet to come! The night vigil with no sleep all night. We had a choice of praying out of doors, round the Stations of the Cross, or in the chapel. We picked the chapel rule for the night vigil. No one was allowed to bundle up or cover their feet, and certainly not to go to sleep. The stewards or Legion of Mary were on duty to wake anyone who did, a duty they performed with an almost malicious glee.

The Rosary was recited all night, a priest in the pulpit intoning the glorious mysteries and the sorrowful mysteries. Most of the bare-footed pilgrims walked around and around the freezing church. At five in the morning, perks—a sermon in Irish! By seven thirty, sheer cruelty: we could smell the aroma of eggs and bacon coming from the priest's house.

The night was over, thanks be to God, and fortified with a breakfast of Lough Derg soup we were ready to face another day. I remember thinking: if I am ever committed to a psychiatric hospital, I will be running around in circles saying Hail Marys over and over. At nine o'clock that evening we were allowed to go to the dormitory for our one night's sleep. We slept on hard wooden bunk beds with two hairy blankets. If I'd been on down in the Shelbourne Hotel I couldn't have been happier. We all slept like the dead.

Our last day dawned and it was time for the final purging; a really good confession! First the body is lashed into submission and then one must suffer the purgation of all those mea culpas. Still reciting the Rosary we joined the long queues for confession. Four Priests were hearing. Mother and I joined (at her advice!) the queue for the older deaf one. She went in ahead of me. One is not supposed to listen but she spoke so loudly that everyone on our bench heard her "It's a year Father," and then "I don't want your absolution, I take my sins upon myself," and I had to go in after that! I was young and believed the priest was representing Christ. The old Monsignor was nice to me and I felt happy and at peace with myself.

So tired, dirty and spiritually purged, we queued at the jetty for our shoes and to board the boats for the mainland. Our feet were so swollen the shoes wouldn't go on and some of the veteran pilgrims had brought a size larger in shoes. Bare-footed we boarded the boats. "Star of the Sea" began again and we all waved back at the island from where the parish priest gave his blessing. Through the muddy field to the buses and finally the train for Dublin.

We settled down. Someone said, "Start the Rosary" and my mother said, "I'll go off my head." Hot water and rye bread were passed around, finally the train drew into Dublin at eight o'clock in the evening. Still bare-footed and carrying our shoes, as were numerous others, we hailed a taxi for home. There was food ready but we were obliged to fast until midnight. Strangely neither Mother or I wanted to eat. We just fell into bed, exhausted.

The next day dawned. I felt disorientated. I had lost eight pounds. My mother said she had found the cure and she kept off the jar for a week.

God moves in mysterious ways. I didn't get my fellow, perhaps because at Lough Derg I had forgotten to pray about him. Years later I found out that he was gay. Spiritual experience, for me, is a feeling of being cleansed, but I was put off feet for life. I studied red ones, blue ones, corns, bunions and hammer toes; everything except a cloven hoof. Perhaps our little trip will help people to understand the funny and sometimes affectionate relationship I had with my mother. When we look back it is seldom we can dislike those we have laughed with. Mother and I had a lot of laughs.

The pilgrimage over, I could not make up my mind what to do with my life, what to study careerwise. I was really a jack of all trades and sadly master of none. As I had shown talent in drawing and painting, Father wanted me to study art in Switzerland, a wonderful offer, but I refused.

15 Hollywood

I was starstruck and my Mother decided that I was to be the next film star in the family. Though I had only a year's drama training and little else except the sheer optimism of youth, Mother and I booked our passage to the U.S.A. I did have some talents but I was fat and only five foot tall, and so I went on a mad starvation diet, eating only cream crackers. It was hell. Of course the press got hold of this piece of gossip and I had photographs taken and we had an enormous farewell party. My dress, made by Miss Manley of Brown Thomas, was three shades of blue chiffon with pink and red roses in velvet. But I looked fatter than ever and I did such a silly thing. I had saved a lot of pink paper rose-buds off party crackers and I pinned eight of them onto the curls on top of my head. I really believed this is it; I'm going places. We had a three piece orchestra and a hundred guests. It was a beautiful night. The moon shone on the sea and the villagers lined the driveway to glimpse the dancers through the big windows. It was a happy and memorable occasion.

So Mother and I left for Hollywood. We travelled by liner from Belfast and had ten wonderful days at sea, though we did run into some rough weather that made me seasick. Every day we were presented with the programme for the day: deck-tennis, swimming, treasure hunts, and at night dancing, and a ship's concert in which I featured: "Piano accordion selected by Miss S O'Sullivan." Everyone sang to the popular tunes, and I did not have to worry about looking po-faced over the top of my accordion!

Father, who was never mean when it came to big occasions, sponsored everything, including trunks full of new and expensive clothes. I was thrilled, on a lovely sunny morning, to get my first glimpse of the Statue of Liberty and the wonderful Manhattan sky-line. When we arrived in New York a yellow cab driver gave us the run around, the city routine, and then dumped us at a "Gays only" hotel. He *had* said "I don't go for the Irish." Next day we boarded the train of the Santa-Fe line that went across California, five nights on the train across the stark desert. Mother and I both suffered from claustrophobia and not being able to open a window made us both panicky, although the train was air conditioned because we were travelling into intense heat.

Half way there, the train halted and we were told not to get out. It was so hot. It was an Indian reservation and the Indians were all in their feathers and beads, I suppose for us tourists. Their beautiful little babies hung on their backs. The Indians boarded the train with trays of turquoise and silver jewellery, all hand-made, and terribly expensive. Finally we arrived at Los Angeles and there was Maureen running down the track. She was heavily pregnant with her first child. She was dressed in black, to disguise her size, and—a clever ploy—to distract from her tum she wore a beautiful hat with a huge white rose. Poor Maureen: expecting her first baby and then having her mother and sister to entertain.

This was my mother's third trip to Hollywood, where she was welcomed as a great personality. She was a wonderful raconteur and could make the simplest story hilarious. The stars of the 1930s meant nothing to her; she remembered only the stars of the silent screen, Lilian Gish, Pola Negri and of course Rudolf Valentino. She hated talking pictures. Mother became pally with Bing Crosby's housekeeper and for ages had told me about this nice woman who ran this marvellous house for a quiet bald-headed man. One day the baldy man gave this huge party for my Mum and he sang "When Irish Eyes are Smiling," especially for her. Mother goes up to Bing and says "You've a nice voice, you ought to be on the pictures." That went down in Hollywood as a classic story and Bing liked it best of all.

I remember one occasion when I was a little girl, that I was thrilled to get a postcard from Hollywood. My mother was staying in a guest house run by Laurel and Hardy. She said they were very thrifty, even mean, with money. They used sit out on the front steps chewing gum. Dismissing these thoughts, I started thinking more of the present. Maureen's limo was awaiting us, with Sam, the black chauffeur-cum-valet, at the wheel. Sam seemed pleased to see Mother again. We had a ten mile drive from Los Angeles to Bel-Air in Hollywood where Maureen and John Farrow lived. Bel-Air was the social equivalent of Beverley Hills. Here the glitterati lived in their Spanish-style houses with patios and large swimming pools.

En route Maureen pointed out places of interest:
The Brown Derby where all the stars dined, and the
Earl Carrols where the most beautiful girls in the
world would saunter down the vast ramp with
glittering feathered head pieces and little else! Then
Graumann's Chinese Theatre where the famous and
the infamous left their footprints in the cement. Later
on I was thrilled to find that my feet fitted Judy
Garland's footprints. I met her in due course.
Graumann's always made me feel I was in a cheerful
cemetery. Then the beautiful outdoor theatre, the
famous Hollywood Bowl. The smell of heat, dust and
flowers, lights glittering everywhere. The car pulled
to a stop. It was Maureen's home, a sprawling
Spanish-style house. The lights were on even around
the swimming pool. The staff stood outside to
welcome us. Lovely gentle black folk, Sam, his wife
Nellie, cordon-bleu cook and Elaine, a pretty little
mulatto maid who was dresser to Maureen. My sister
lived like a star with everything money could buy.

I did not envy Maureen her lifestyle. I thought her
beautiful and deserving of such a setting. But she
made me feel depressingly inferior. From the start I
was afraid of John Farrow, while recognising his
charm and glamour. I though him autocratic and
domineering. He was, and remained, very fond of
Mother, and would ask his friends to the house just to
hear her raucous stories of life in Ireland. That plus the
fact that no person, place, or thing ever intimidated
her. She was a law unto herself.

Maureen, aged twenty-eight, was at the zenith of
her career. Apart from *Song of My Heart*, her first film,
she had made three of the Tarzan of the Apes series,
The Big Clock, with Charles Laughton, *A Day at the*

Races with the Marx brothers, and had played the part of Dora in *David Copperfield*. She had a contract with MGM for three more films in the Tarzan series for as soon as her baby was born.

John Farrow, too, was a busy man. He had completed his large volumes *A Pageant of the Popes* and *Damien the Leper*. John had lived on the Island of Molokai with the lepers while writing the book. He described how the chieftain of the island insisted on giving him his own bed to sleep in, the only bed on the island. When he later discovered that the chieftain was a leper, John frantically scoured his body with red soap and pumice!

John was made a Papal Knight by Pope Pius XII for his book on Father Damien. He was very interested in Roman Catholicism and prior to meeting Maureen he had been a lapsed Catholic for years. He had been married to a Jewess and he had a daughter by his first marriage. The Church granted an annullment on the grounds that a marriage between a Jew and a Christian was simply not recognised but it took five years for the Church to finalise this decision. John and Maureen's house was always full of priests, bishops and Archbishop Cantwell of Los Angeles, who always travelled with his own entourage, his big masculine sister Nellie, and always three paces behind, like Uriah Heep, a weedy be-spectacled priest, his secretary. When they came to dine we wore black frocks with high necks. His Grace told Mother that he didn't believe Maureen had ever even committed a venial sin! Such a load of bull! Mother's retort was, "Maureen can be as big a fiend as the rest of them." One of John's earlier literary efforts was kept hidden from us. My father had locked it in his safe but one day he left the safe open and I had a quick read through *Laughter Ends*, a book about Polynesian prostitutes. Mother said if we sent it to the Pope he would take away John's Papal title.

Maureen and John told me to lose a stone in weight (I was five foot and weighed 8st 8lbs), to grow my plucked eyebrows, grow my hair and not get too sun-tanned in the Californian sun because it did not come over too well on camera. I was to be groomed for a film test. The dieting was hard. John Farrow kept jeering at me and repeating "Maureen, can you imagine Sheila acting with Weissmuller?" The ridicule was absurd because nobody would have been idiotic enough to cast a man as huge as Weissmuller with a woman as tiny as me. My Dublin clothes looked far from smart in Hollywood. Whenever we were dining out I used hear John call "Maureen, why don't you have Elaine bring down some clothes to your mother and sister!" So we usually went out bedecked in Maureen's finery.

I was a nuisance, Maureen finally told me. We did not have rows, just that once she really let me have it. She said it was no time for me to come out to America and expect her to launch me socially, when she was expecting a child. She said I was sulky, unappreciat-ive, that I was like an aunt of ours whom she detested, Aunt Ned, my father's little pianist sister. Maureen went on and on I said nothing. I couldn't because my idol was tottering on her pedestal. Mother intervened on my behalf. You see what Maureen did not know, nor did I, was that I was not quiet because I was sulking. I was depressed. At home it didn't show because no one talked much to me anyway, but here amid the glitter and high-pitched animation I stood out like a sore thumb.

To accustom me to the feel of film sets, Maureen arranged a grand tour of the Metro Goldwyn Mayer

Studios for Mother and me. Our first stop was the office of the great Louis B. Mayer himself, a fat pleasant man never without an expensive cigar in his mouth. I met many of the stars of the late thirties, like dear old Barry Fitzgerald, Judy Garland and Mickey Rooney. Mickey and Judy were making a film called *Babes in Arms*. I thought Rooney a cocky little brat, all five foot of him. He was talking to me and telephoning to his man servant, "see my tuxedo is left ready for me." Judy was sweet and attending school on the lot. She was too fat as well and was already on the amphetamines which were later to be a serious health hazard. At lunch in the studio canteen I was introduced to Clark Gable, so charming and so handsome. He was eating a large salad. He shook hands with me, and said, "Welcome to Hollywood, honey," and honey went weak at the knees and couldn't utter one bloody word!

I saw a number of very plastic looking stars and starlets. They all wore these terrible uplift bras and there was a big to-do about buying these. Everyone who was anyone went for at least two fittings to the bra shop. If one was a film star, of course the lady came to the house. Maureen arranged that the "bra lady" come to fit Mother and me. She made such a fuss about it and said we were both a bit floppy. In Ireland busts were there but not flaunted. My mother and I were both fairly well endowed. The shop lady explained that we would need two bras each: for day wear, she said, one wore a "round" but well-separated uplift, for night or dress wear, not the rounded look but "points" like twin guns. Mother and I laughed our heads off. We felt enormous in our new bras and I died a thousand deaths every time I had to take off my coat. I thought my twin guns were pointing at every man in the room. Consequently I often refused to remove my coat and nearly died from the heat.

However, living as I was on a starvation diet, I was gradually losing weight. I was introduced to Freddie Bartholomew who was no longer a wimpish little Lord Fauntleroy but a big handsome chap. His Aunt Cissie used to follow us everywhere. She was a bloody nuisance. But we did manage a few dates and we used to go to the bowling alley. All the younger stars went there and it was full of gossip columnists, reporters and radio newsmen. One came up to Freddie and me, microphone in hand, and said with the usual nasal brashness, "Hi folks, this is down town Hollywood, the bowling alley. Maureen O'Sullivan's sister Sheila is dating Freddie Bartholomew. She is over from Ireland and under contract to MGM." I wasn't under any contract and I felt very embarrassed.

I had never seen anything like the lifestyle of those stars. Hollywood in the late thirties was at its peak and the stars themselves were publicised like gods and goddesses. I knew nothing of the heartbreaks and scandals. I was told that Louis B Mayer, head of MGM, kept stables at the studios and on a visit there I said to the great Mr Mayer, "Can I go and look at your horses?" He looked amazed and said, "We're not shooting a movie with horses." I made things worse. I said, "I was told you had stables." I could see by his face that he understood something I didn't. Aapparently the expression was derived from all the little starlets or would-be stars who slept with him hoping for parts in movies.

Hollywood was full of beautiful people—in the stores, drive-ins, gas stations—all hoping to be seen or discovered. Women spent a fortune on themselves: the gym for figures, hours in the beauty parlour and virtually everyone had perfect white capped teeth. Mother remarked that they were "a neurotic awful crowd, full of vanity and jealousy." This was in one of her lucid moments. At one of the "come for a swim and tennis after" parties, in the palatial home of one Dorothy Jordan, the hostess showed us her bedroom. It was like a shop and all her outfits were catalogued. I counted fifty pairs of shoes, for starters. Mother *had* to go and say, "All we have is two pairs, one on and one off."

Hollywood was tennis crazy and most of the stars were pros at the game. I had been dreading the tennis session. I looked the part in my short white skirt and super racquet but I missed every ball and hit my partner, cowboy star Nick Foran, on the back of the head with a tennis ball. My service went astray! Maureen and John were furious. They said I'd no business to say I could play and that all these people were professionals! I hadn't much going for me other than the optimism of youth. At eighteen I was totally overwhelmed by my new surroundings. John Farrow kept jeering at me. I felt very unhappy and inadequate. I wonder if he meant to do that.

I went to one big soirée given for Larry Adler, the famous harmonica player, to celebrate his thirtieth birthday. All the glitterati were there; it was like a colour movie. I saw Ronald Reagan and his then wife Jane Wyman (he has changed remarkably little), Ginger Rogers, Merle Oberon, Doris Day, Orson Welles, Judy Garland, I have all their signatures in my famous autograph album. I was learning fast. After four months in Hollywood I was not as naive as when I arrived. One producer, who was to fix me up with a film test, took me out to dinner and after the meal we strolled in the grounds of the hotel. Then the interview started: "What shape are your breasts, close together or far apart?" We were sitting on a seat in the garden. I moved away a bit. "Was I a virgin?" He moved over. "Now your legs. I'd better feel them to know the shape—unless you'd like to lift up your skirt." I told him, "You are a fat, ugly and filthy old man!" I was amazed that he gave me a film test, but nothing came of it! I didn't think anything would. Mother was quite unimpressed by everything and everyone, and I sensed she was getting fidgety to go back to Ireland.

I finally went for my film test. I was seven stone, I had lost a stone and a half, my hair had grown shoulder length, and my eyebrows too had grown. My test was shot solo although Maureen said it was easier with another actor. I'd had to learn a monologue from the play *Stage Door*. The original had been filmed in 1937 with Katherine Hepburn and Lucille Ball, and was a story about the heartbreak of would-be actresses. My piece was one girl's speech on leaving the theatrical boarding house. She was saying good-bye sadly and tearfully to her friends; she had become hard enough to chuck it all and go and marry her old sugar daddy. It was an emotional and depressing speech and it took twelve minutes to recite! I was hours in make-up. I decided there must be a lot wrong with my face if they took so long to recreate it. I wore a simple black dress to show off the new figure, with a big white lace collar. I was dead nervous and I was surprised when everyone clapped. Later Maureen, Mother and I saw my test in a tiny cinema where they showed rushes. I went back, still covered in make-up, to Maureen's house. I was really elated because the director had told Maureen it was a good test.

In a sense the days were idyllic, swimming in the pool, sunbathing, visiting all the famous places, meeting the rich and ambitious, especially having the figure to wear nice clothes. But all the time my mind was in a turmoil. There were no calls from my agent or the film studios. Was I going to be sent home a failure? I had left to such a fanfare.

Mother decided we were too much for Maureen and John and we moved to a very grotty apartment in downtown Hollywood. It was hideous and hideously expensive. There was one main room, a kitchenette off, no bath, just a shower, and of course no garden. I hated it; it smelt of dry dust and cement. The worst part was our beds, two doors, out of which, when they were opened, crashed two Murphy beds. I thought it would take an Irishman to invent them. They either stuck or crashed!

Maureen used send Sam the chauffeur down to us with fresh fruit and vegetables. Still no news from the studios and Mother kept saying she was "dying to go home." I remember lying in bed and looking up at the myriad lights that were Hollywood, city of broken dreams and broken hearts, and I cried and cried because I knew my dream was over. I had just been allowed to have a look at all that might have been. The news was ominous: war clouds were gathering over Europe. Finally Maureen went into hospital to have the baby. John, my Mother and I hung about the labour room and we could hear Maureen saying, "it's torture, it's torture." Then I heard the baby cry for the first time. The doctor opened the door and said to John, "You have a son." The baby was baptised Michael Damien (after Fr Damien the leper priest) and everyone was very happy.

About a week after Maureen returned home with her baby, Mother left and went home to Ireland. I was dreadfully upset, I had often wished she would go home, but when she did I missed her. It was always like that. There was still no news from the studios and meanwhile Maureen had an offer to make a film in England, *A Busman's Holiday* with Robert Montgomery. I had left the awful apartment Mother and I shared and I was quite settled in Maureen's lovely home, and of course I loved the baby. I was very apprehensive: would Maureen go to England, what about me? Obviously John Farrow wouldn't want to look after a teenage hopeful, I could no longer impose on them and I was too young to be left alone in Hollywood. I was heartbroken. Freddie (Bartholomew) and his bloody Aunt Cissie came to say goodbye. When they had gone I sat there with the tears rolling down my face. A knock at the door. Freddie (alone): "I forgot my sunglasses." He kissed me and that, for what it was worth, was that. He was crying too. Remembering happy times when one is lonely is soul-destroying.

Maureen and I were to sail on the famous *Queen Mary*. She was truly wonderful and beautiful. I remember going to shop in Piccadilly Circus on board the ship. We were invited to many functions, including cocktails with the Captain and First Officer. Dancing every night and everything to do. During the day one could even hire bicycles to pedal along and see the vast ship. But the fact remained, my heart was heavy. I was going home a failure.

One night we were summoned to the main lounge to hear a broadcast by the Prime Minister. I will never forget those words, "We are now at war with Nazi

Germany." It was 3 September 1939. Everyone was strained and subdued. The great ship was blacked out that night, not a light showing anywhere. It was eerie to peep through a porthole. On either side of the great ship we had a destroyer escort, also blacked out and gliding silently along. Happily the great ship arrived at Southampton without mishap. I was dreading meeting the press. Maureen told me to say I'd come home to do a year's study with the Abbey Theatre. Fortunately, the press were far more interested in her than in me! We spent a few days in London, at the Dorchester, while Maureen saw movie people about her film, which, it turned out, was to be cancelled. We took my nice Aunt Maud from Hampstead out to dinner. It was high living, but for me it was nearly over.

I went back home to my beloved Saintbury and no Hollywood home could hold a candle to that mellowed and lovely old house.

16

Dances and Parties

Father said to me, "You are a flop, you are a flop at everything you do." I felt so bad I wished I was dead. It hurt, it really hurt and it was true. Maureen stayed at home for a while but she was anxious to get back home to her husband and baby. Mother said it was only natural. Father was fretting because Maureen had to go back to America. He loved her so much, I think he was jealous of her husband. He was lonely and she showed him love and affection. For some reason I couldn't show anyone love or affection, not even my brother or sisters. I always felt they didn't like me that much. Father said if John was ever unfaithful to Maureen he personally would shoot him. Mother's reply was, "don't be ridiculous, Charlie."

My father and mother were totally unsuited. Why did he make an alcoholic woman pregnant six times? She was incapable of taking care of us. Each one of us has been affected by their disastrous marriage in different ways. Maureen went back to the States.

Father worried about Jack, my brother, who was then a captain in the King's Own Royal Regiment. Ireland was neutral and Father ranted and shouted about these "damned neutrals." Mother said, "We'd better have a party to cheer us up." As usual Father was told, "We're only having twenty-five couples," a mere fifty people. That always placated him but we invited a hundred guests. The drawing room floor had stood up to so many dances that Mother, acting on someone's advice, called in an architect, a good friend of mine, to check it. He gave the floor and ceiling below (Father's study) the OK—quite safe. Mother as usual booked Father into a Dun Laoghaire hotel for the night. A shame really, because once he got over the usual fracas—"these damned parties"—he was a good host, liked the pretty girls and enjoyed himself.

This time Mother decided to smarten up the place before the dance. She painted all the window sills inside the drawing room white the day before. Then she painted my father's bath—his bathroom was en-suite. The bath was very big and rusty with a brown wooden rim, like a sarcophagus. Above was the gas geyser that heated the water with terrifying chortling noises and emitted gushes of brown rusty water. There were blue marks on the bath. Mother said it was a "most depressing bathroom" and "he is so un-romantic with all his horrible cosmetics." These were in the brown cupboard under the wash basin: a bottle of Milton, a spare set of heavy dentures in a black box, Lifebuoy soap. A shelf underneath held his commode, gold rimmed with poppies, and a bottle of Jeyes Fluid—the commode was put back under his bed by Essie, the parlour maid, at nine-thirty in the evening.

Father ran his bath and got in but he didn't know

the paint was still tacky. The shouts and roars of him! "I wouldn't doubt you, you damned fool of a woman," he bellowed. He had lain down in the bath and his outline was preserved in mosaic for posterity!

Father footed the bill for these parties. He paid for the food and the drink but he would not pay for the band or the hired piano. He always locked away our own beautiful piano pianola when there was a party, and I had to pawn my diamond bracelet to foot the bill for the music.

We had an indoor staff of three and Nanny and Mrs West, the gardener's wife, to help out at these parties. However this time Mother decided to hire a waiter, to hand out drinks. He was a funny shabby little man called Finch, but he flew round with the drinks well enough. But after the ball was over, we found him out for the count on the dining room floor. With the help of four strong young men Finch was put to bed in a small room near the kitchen. The dance went off wonderfully well. I was then nineteen, Pat five years younger than me and Betty only eleven. They were both already pretty, Pat, the only blue-eyed blonde in our family, already developing the great figure she became known for. Betty was small and dark and still only a child. How could I have a relationship with them with these age gaps? I was fond of little Betty but I always felt that Pat did not approve of me. Perhaps I was too much like Mother. Maureen and Jackie were away, and I really only got to know them through letter writing.

At about ten o'clock on the morning after the dance, we were all woken up by a terrible crash and the sound of masonry falling. Out of our bedrooms we came. Mother shouted cheerfully enough, "We've been bombed by the Germans." The drawing-room ceiling had caved in and sixty pounds of concrete had fallen on the settee in my father's study. It kept falling in lumps and the hired piano shot through the big hole and crashed with almighty discord! Luckily, our own piano was in the bay window where the floor was still intact! Mother said, "It's lucky I am a sensible woman and sent your father away, or he could be lying under all that concrete."

There was hell to pay when Father came back, but Mother reasoned (she did at times reason) that if it had happened during the dance how very much worse it would have been. Finch, the hired waiter, didn't waken for two days. At one stage Mother said he was dead because there was an awful smell in the room. "What," she said, "will we do with him if he's dead?" "Bury him with Minnie," someone suggested. Minnie was our old cat.

17   The WAAF

Parties and all, boredom set in and caused me to do another stupid thing. I would join the WAAF, the Women's Royal Air Force. The year was 1940 and I was twenty years old. There were fifty-two trades to choose from. What about driving an MT (motor transport) lorry? Me, five foot and seven stone? I went to Belfast with a couple of friends to enrol. Of course they quashed the lorry idea. We were all smallish girls and the three of us were enrolled as RDF operators (Radar Direction Finding). We had to swear an oath of secrecy because this was war and we were dealing with a new secret weapon still unknown to the Germans. Requirements were a good education, good speaking voice, cool nerves, excellent eye sight. We were of course duly tested for all these. They didn't say a good standard of maths. They should have. That was my weak point. After the tests we went home to await the call-up papers.

My papers arrived telling me to report at RAF, Bridgnorth, the WAAF initial training centre, ten days from then. Mother decided on a farewell dinner-party for me. There were fourteen guests at the table. For once my father was proud of me and gave me all sorts of tips, like wearing puttees to keep my legs warm. He told me the soldiers in the trenches in 1914 wore them. These were rolls of material wound round from ankle to knee. Great for keeping warm but I though I would rather be cold!

My friend Judy and I left from Belfast by boat and stayed overnight in London. A changed London with air raid shelters everywhere and the whole city blacked out after dark. We were issued with travel warrants so that we travelled everywhere free. Next day we were to travel by train to Shropshire. Bridgnorth was our destination for kitting out and for our initial training. We got off the train at nine o'clock at night, to be greeted, or should I say shouted at, by horrible looking women wearing the WAAF uniform, Air Force blue, a corporal's two stripes on the sleeve. We must have very obviously looked a lost bunch of girls, because one of the corporals yelled in our direction,"You lot over there, all rookies, go to the trucks outside the station." We were tired and it was a very cold month of January in 1941. I lumped along with my huge round hat-box, full of useless things like pretty undies though we had been told to bring the minimum of luggage. Judy and I and some others from Dublin clambered into one of the trucks. After a long silent drive in the black dark sitting on hard wooden benches, we arrived in the dark to our blacked-out camp. The entire vast camp was disguised so that it looked like a chicken farm from the air; all the huts were black and spattered with white. This was RAF Bridgnorth.

We were shouted at through megaphones and told

the way to go. We had to show a tin-hatted soldier our ID cards at the gate. Orders were being bellowed out: "Before being allocated to your sleeping quarters, all rookies will march—march mind you!—to hut 97 for FFI." What the hell is FFI, I wondered? We entered a long building with harsh naked bulbs swinging and about twelve hard-faced females in white coats and rubber gloves awaiting us. Another order was bellowed through the megaphone: "This is the free-from-infection unit. You are all to be checked for head lice." One of the Dublin girls, Jane, was an exceptionally beautiful blonde with glorious hair. They told her that they had found a dead nit in her hair, so at that hour of the night, they soaked her beautiful hair in paraffin and didn't even dry it for her. Poor Jane was hysterical. I was next. "Come over here, Paddy"—all Irish were Paddy—"Did you bring any bugs over from Dublin?" I felt like socking her between the eyes. She was a stocky woman with black hair cropped short, a slight moustache and muscular legs. She smiled with her teeth and her eyes remained cold. "Now sit there" (the chair under the swinging light bulb). She raked the steel fine-comb over my scalp.

Judy, my friend, was getting worried that we might be separated. It was a huge camp divided up into north, south, east and west zones. Our orders were once more being bellowed out: "All Irish rookies to west camp. Corporal Fountain will march you over and show you your huts." Our glamorous acquaintance Jane was still crying because her hair was stinking with paraffin. We had to line up in twos, carrying our luggage and it had started to snow. Corporal Fountain called out, "at the ready, quick march, left, left, left right left, try and keep in step, you're going to have to, from now on."

The sleeping quarters were Nissen huts, 36 women to each hut with dreadful beds. The mattresses were called biscuits because they comprised three hard flat cushions. There was just enough room for a locker between each bed and no privacy at all. There was a stone fireplace dead centre with a big chimney reaching up through the roof. Luckily Judy and I were in the same hut. A bossy black woman called Johnnie, a right bitch, immediately established herself as hut leader. She immediately named Judy and myself, "the Irish aristocracy in the corner." We were all too tired and too cold to take much interest in the people round us. Our beds were not made up. The bedding was folded in a neat pile at the end of each bed and at the top were two pillows. There was a pillow case but no sheets. We were briefed by Corporal Fountain that when not in use, the beds must always be left in that order. She was to be in charge of our hut. She was tall, thin and dark with a cockney accent, which she tried to hide. She never smiled and we were to learn to dislike her thoroughly.

That first night we slept like the dead. We were called at 6 am by reveille, a blast of bugles through the amplifier, followed by Corporal Fountain's march through the hut as she shouted, "Up everybody on the double to the wash house. Dress, stack your bedding and I'll march you over to the cookhouse for breakfast. You have exactly twenty minutes." The long washroom with stone floors and lavatories off was horrible. Nearly all the plugs were missing, there were paper towels and no soap. Soap was rationed and precious and most of the Irish had forgotten to bring soap. The bathrooms were as bad, the only decent ones for corporals only.

It was still dark with wet snow on the ground as we were marched over to the cookhouse. We hadn't been kitted out with our uniforms yet and we looked a right motley crew. We were told to line up outside the cookhouse and "each of you will be issued with a knife, fork and spoon. Don't lose them or you will have to eat with your fingers!" The cook house was enormous with long wooden tables seating twelve on either side. The catering officer (at all meals) would wander up and down shouting "Any complaints?" There were very few. The food was extraordinarily good, considering the catering was on such an enormous scale. Breakfast was porridge, egg and bacon. Lunch was soup, meat, two veg and pudding. Tea was buns, cakes and fruit. Twice during the morning and afternoon we could queue up for a mug of cocoa and a doughnut. We all got disgustingly fat. Then at our own expense we could buy coffees, sweets and cigarettes at the NAAFI and Salvation Army canteens in the compound.

On that first day we were marched to the stores to be fitted out. Warm Air Force blue greatcoat, worn over a jacket with RAF buttons, skirt, blue shirt and black tie. The caps were a bit like mushrooms with a black peak, crowned by our WAAF badge. Except for the cap and skirt our uniform was the same as the men and of course the WAAF on transport wore slacks.

We wore thick grey stockings and sensible black shoes, wool vests and black directoire knickers, known as "service black-outs." We were disgusted with the undies. Little did we know how grateful we would be, as the cold in Shropshire was really something so much colder than Ireland.

Of course when we progressed a bit, we had our uniforms tailored to fit and for service dances we wore nylons. Regulations were many; a strict one was that hair had to be worn two inches above the collar. We were inspected every day, buttons polished, shoes gleaming. I took pride in my appearance and was delighted when the officer inspecting us pointed me out as a model WAAF. All our worldly goods went into a kit bag which was carried hitched over the shoulder. Mine was bigger than me. It was also compulsory at all times to carry a gas mask. I thought of the silly round hat-box full of flimsy frivolous undies and make up. Until I could get rid of it I had to lug it round. I was bowed down with all the luggage and finally I sent the box to my Aunt in London.

After breakfast each day, we had to go back to our huts, pile up the bedding and polish the lino in the floor space between the beds. I hated doing it. After chores, square-bashing began. Dad's army was only in the halfpenny place. On the barrack square endless marching arms swinging to shoulder height "left, left, left right, left." I could hear it in my sleep. Then there were the dreaded route marches. We'd march the ten miles, then some of us couldn't make it back and were allowed to return on the bus. We all suffered torture with our feet.

We had to salute every officer, male or female, and if we were carrying parcels and couldn't salute we gave an "eyes right." Some of us became quite adept at this and at times it was a bit of a giggle. We all wore two IDs around our necks with name, religion and number. One of mine said O'Sullivan 053 and the other Roman Catholic in case we were killed in a raid. Testing the gas masks was something everyone dreaded. We all had to put on our masks and then enter a hut full of tear gas in twos. If the masks were not A1, that was no joke. Sometimes we had mock air raids. The sirens would start wailing and tear-gas was let loose all over the camp. God help the one who had no mask. The coughing and the sore eyes lasted quite a while too.

If we had any money (ten shillings a week was pay for rookies) we'd go to any of the pubs in Bridgnorth, always full of service personnel, or we'd go to dances in other parts of the camp. These were held in huge aerodrome hangars. I had long hair and I got into trouble for letting it down at the dance. I was reported to Sergeant Pim. "You are to work as an ACHGD for one week, O'Sullivan." This was the lowest form of life in the Airforce, air craft hand general duties, and that meant anything from running messages and peeling mountains of potatoes to cleaning rows of lavatories.

Every week we all lined up for pay parade. We had to march up to the table, salute the officer in charge and say "053 O'Sullivan Sir," collect the ten shillings and right about turn.

On Sundays we had obligatory church parade. Everyone assembled on the barrack square and the Protestant padre on the rostrum would call loud and clear through a megaphone, "Jews and Roman Catholics fall out and face the wall," which we did while all the others recited the Lord's Prayer. In the nineteen forties Roman Catholics were strictly forbidden to participate in any service other than their own. Then we all had to march to the Protestant Church where we fell out again and the Catholics went to Mass.

The Catholic padre was a really nice man who took me especially under his wing, I expect because I am small and I looked even less than my twenty years. He wanted someone to play the mini-organ. Fool that I was, I volunteered. I really thought that because I could play the piano and the piano-accordion that it would be no problem. So I turned up for Sunday Mass. The large church was crowded. I sat down at the organ and the music was put in front of me. I glanced at it; no problem. It was easy to read, but all the stops! I pulled out one and nothing happened. Then I tried another and produced a noise like a cow mooing. The choir went on singing, while I produced the most terrible noises. At that solemn moment, the consecration of the Mass, it had become a cacophony, so I took to my heels and ran. I was so ashamed. When the priest sent for me I was scared stiff. He was also an officer and I felt sure he would put me on a charge, as well as giving me a proper telling off. But no, he could not have been kinder. He said, "I was so sorry for you, it must have been awful."

The town of Bridgnorth was attractive and quaint. It comprised a high town and low town, connected by a funicular railway and a flight of steps. One night I drank a sailor's rum ration and the sailor and I ran, or flew, down virtually hundreds of steep steps in the black of night. There I met and fell in love with a young naval officer, Lieutenant John Reeves. Such a sad and silly thing happened. He got a posting to go to sea on active service and we were to write to each other. I gave him the wrong address because after a few gins I was confused. I never heard from him again. Even now I remember. I wonder does he!

We were only supposed to stay in Bridgnorth camp for three weeks' initial training. It seemed they were not ready for us at RAF Cranwell where we radio operators were to be trained, so it turned into three pretty tough months. Finally the posting came and I was glad that my friend Judy was to be sent with me.

Cranwell in Lincolnshire was much better than the camp at Bridgnorth, but we were still billeted in the same awful huts, 36 to a hut. However the washrooms and baths were much better. I chose a bed in a corner. Written on the wall over my bed was, "Spud Murphy slept here." Another poor bloody Irish fool, I wrote underneath, "and O'Sullivan 053 slept here too."

The RDF (as it was always called) or Radio Direction Finding course started immediately. It all went on underground, because the machines were secret and hidden and the work was carried on in the dark. The only light was on the radar screens themselves. This was television in its infancy. The operator used a control called a gonio, a knob you turned gently from left to right, right to left, sweeping across the screen and enemy aircraft came in as dots of light. The gonio picked them out and we gave a position reading from the machine sounding like "AF (aircraft) nina fife (ninety five) zero fife (05)." This was phoned through to the girls in the plotting room, who got a final position and then sent that on to the ACK (girls on gun sites who were given orders to "shoot down enemy aircraft." To the lay person it sounded like double Dutch, but it worked with marvellous precision.

This was 1941 and America had come into the war. The big news at Cranwell was that the Yanks had arrived, their slogan "over paid, over sexed and over here." The dance halls and pubs were taken over by gum chewing GIs in thin monkey-jacket uniforms with caps tipped over their noses. They were different—extrovert, brash and in the money. They wooed the girls with candy, cigarettes and nylons. On the more negative side our administrative officers gave us lectures on how to protect ourselves when walking back to the camp at night in the black-out. Always walk in a group, never alone, carry hat pins girls, and if you have to, use them. We quite often did!

I wasn't a bad radio operator, but the classes upset me. They were thoroughly mathematical and I have always had a block about maths. During a trial run, my friend Judy and I had plotted and reported enemy aircraft coming in, location position and height. They were not German planes but RAF squadrons. Had it been for real we would have ordered our own to be shot down!

I knew it was coming. ASO Cherry House, who was in charge of our unit, sent for me. Though she was young she was intimidating, typical of the English upper class. She said, "At ease, O'Sullivan" (I was not) and, "Look, I feel despite the utter carelessness during the trial exercises you have it in you, you have the makings of a jolly good radio op. and I am going to give you a second chance." The second chance did no good. Both my friend Judy and I had become paranoid and we were so afraid of having the wrong aircraft shot down that we never acquired the necessary calm required for that skilled job and we were both taken off the course. Until we decided on another trade we were both A.C.H.G.D.s, aircraft hand general duties, cookhouse and lavatories again.

My twenty-first birthday was approaching. I had looked forward to going home for this, but owing to heavy air raids all leave was stopped. I was very depressed. The cold in Lincolnshire was brutal. I developed acute bronchitis and had endless colds. Working in the dark, squinting at dots of light on radar screens had affected my eyes. The conjunctivitis was so bad that I'd bathe my eyes open in the morning. All my eyelashes fell out, so with inflamed pink rims my Irish eyes were no longer twinkling. One had to be really ill to be excused from chores and routine. We had these dreaded route marches every day and keep fit classes in an aerodrome hanger. Our outfit for this was so terrible! We wore our blue shirts and long black drawers, the service black-outs. An RAF bloke playing a saxophone provided the music, a red faced RAF Sergeant-Major gym master bellowed at us and we jumped about looking and feeling bloody awful. Any RAF personnel passing by made it worse because the chaps whistled and shouted at us.

In a sense social life was a whirl because we were all young and because we lived our lives one day at a time. The fact of our all being in uniform broke down class barriers. There was esprit-de-corps and were were proud to have the name of our respective countries on our uniform. The English could not have been nicer or kinder to all service personnel. We were always being invited into people's homes for cups. The Church of England padre practically adopted me, a little Irish Roman Catholic, and I had Sunday lunch with him and his family as a routine. The tough side of things was getting used to, maybe falling in love a bit with some really nice RAF boy and then seeing his name posted up after he had been shot down in the course of duty. There were many tears shed.

My twenty-first birthday came around and we celebrated by eating powered eggs in a café. The sirens went off and we had an air raid. We finished the powdered eggs under the table! When we got back to our hut there was a surprise. The thirty-five women in our hut had planned a birthday party. They had saved their chocolate and sweets rations and drank my health in cocoa.

I couldn't make up my mind up which out of the fifty-two trades in the WAAF to try next. I had a vague idea about becoming a parachute packer, but when I visited the big hangar I was put off immediately by a large notice that read, "remember one wrong fold can cost a man's life." I had had no idea how big a parachute was, lying open on the ground. It took fifteen girls to pack one parachute. That was not for me. Next I tried being a dental assistant. I hated it. While this indecision lasted I had become that lowest of the low, an ACHGD, aircraft hand general duties, for the third time round. I was used mostly as a runner to carry messages from north to east camp and so on. All the time it was "on the double Paddy." At this point, to my joy, I was sent for and told I had two weeks leave on grounds of debilitated health.

Father met me at Dun Laoghaire pier (he said Kingstown till the day he died). It was great to step off the boat on to neutral soil. No black out or bombs and plenty of everything. I had got fat from all the stodgy food but I was in poor health.

Saintbury was waiting for me. As ever, my dog Billy rushed out to greet me and Nanny too. At this stage of my life we were good friends. Pat and Betty, my sisters, were out. Pat was sixteen and Betty thirteen. Pat was a boarder at the Sacred Heart Convent, Mount Anville, in Dundrum. The following year Betty would go too, so this was poor Nanny's last year with us. She cried bitterly and begged to stay on for nothing. She said she would look after the linen but Father was adamant. He said, "That damned old woman will have to go, I'll have no hangers on." She had brought up two of his children and had virtually saved my sister Betty's life. Betty was the baby of the family and before she was born Mother was on a bad drinking spree; the baby weighed five pounds and doctors were dubious about her survival. Nanny had begged for a chance to bring on the baby. The maternity nurse was let go. Father thought there was little hope but the baby survived. Nannie was given a gold watch but no bonus when she left and nothing in Father's will. Betty of course preferred Nanny to Mother, and so did Pat. Maureen and Jack obviously were on Father's side. Someone had to care for Mother, so it seemed it had to be me.

Father actually seemed to take an interest in me. Over dinner my first night home he talked, which was most unusual for him. Mother was half shot so I waited till the morning to talk to her. She was nice in the mornings when she was sober, and very amusing. Father talked about serving with the Connaught Rangers in the Boer War of 1899—1902 when he was a very young subaltern. He showed me a picture of himself outside his block house which the soldiers built themselves. He looked very young and handsome. He said the happiest days of his life were spent alone in the barren vastness of the South African veldt, his only companions his horse, his Great Dane and a little marmoset. He spoiled that story by adding that on hearing the Boers were advancing he had to shoot the horse, his dog and the dear little monkey. He said the Boers would have slaughtered them. There was an awful loneliness in Father which I could feel that night. Mother interrupted by saying in a jeering way, "We're still fighting the Boer War, I fight one every day."

The armistice between Father and me was soon to come to an end. I did not want to go back to Cranwell, so I tried to delay telling Father by capitalising on the health aspect. I felt bad about it, specially when

Mother told me, "He did take such an interest in your letters." I went to an eye specialist and he gave me a note for Cranwell stating that I needed three weeks' more leave. I had two weeks' leave to correct my eye infection. Next an ear and throat specialist. I had septic tonsils; they would have to come out. Another month added on.

I went into hospital for the operation. The tonsillectomy was agony. I had no idea it could be so painful. It was a Dublin hospital and the surgeon was a friend of my father. So pain and all, I did feel secure, until one day when I was out of bed looking for something, a pair of hands encircled my upper half (I hadn't heard him coming) and I was aware of hot breath on the back of my neck. "You are a plump wee girl," said my doctor. I was surprised to find out he was such a rotten groper. I turned on him. I said, "don't you dare touch me!" He went scarlet, and at once became rather cross and said, "I have come in here to look at your throat." I didn't tell Father; he would not have believed me anyway.

My eyes and general health picked up and it was time for me to go back to duty. I told Mother I was not going back to Cranwell. She told Father, and there was bloody murder. My father said that I had taken an oath to King and country. I would be a deserter and of course if I crossed the border into Northern Ireland, the SPs (special police) would arrest me. Happily for me, a big brown envelope arrived with my official discharge from the WAAF. Reason for discharge was given as "Services no longer required," followed by "no medals, clasps or decorations," but, and this saved the day for me, I got "the highest award for conduct and character that the RAF could award while serving on this unit." That mollified my Father for a while. But soon he was to say again to me, "you're a flop at everything you do, a failure." There were times when I hated him—even still I hate him at times—and yet I needed his approval, possibly because all the people who had his approval, especially Maureen and my brother Jack, were people I would have liked to be like. I admired them and their positive approach to life, which seemed sadly lacking in me.

I often wondered why Mother should never be blamed, and why I too didn't rate forgiveness!

18

Leading a Waster's Life

After this episode my Father withdrew from me. In one more utterly futile bid to please him, I agreed to do a course of shorthand and typing at the well known Miss Galway's Secretarial College in Dawson Street with my youngest sister Betty. This flourished in the nineteen forties as a stop-gap for the daughters of the well-to-do, to train them for a job until they eventually married. The ones who didn't were at least equipped for a career. At this stage my sister Pat, who had left school, was working in a firm of accountants. I hated Miss Galway's. It was like going back to school and I could not master the shorthand. I had a friend who did my shorthand homework for me, and this proved to be my undoing. The Principal sent for me. "Your shorthand is quite correct, Miss O'Sullivan," she said, "but what I do not understand is that the method used is Gregg, and we only teach Pitman in this college." A letter was sent to my father recommending my removal: "she mitches classes, is inattentive and has not aptitude for her shorthand." Betty went on with the course and got a good secretarial job.

I didn't know what to do. I had now become convinced that I was a failure and that whatever I did, I would only make a mess of it. So life became a series of boyfriends and parties. The parties in the big Killiney houses were really something. Prior to them people called and left their cards. If my father approved, Mother would return the call and leave her card. Father always insisted that Mother chaperone me but she was such fun (if she wasn't too drunk) that I enjoyed her company. One of the big occasions was the annual fancy dress ball given by Mrs McAteer Parnell and her sister Miss McAteer. They were very old ladies, ninety-one and eighty-nine respectively. The two old ladies wore wigs and masses of make-up and glittering fake jewellery. Mrs Parnell often spoke to me of Charles Stewart. "Dear boy," she'd say, "he was a compulsive talker, and into the early hours of the morning." Another lovely home we were invited to regularly was Boley in Monkstown where Sir Valentine Grace continued to give his quite famous, impromptu musical evenings after the death of his wife. In his youth he had been one of the early actors to grace the Abbey Theatre. He was a huge fat man with beetling eyebrows and a most sonorous voice. He was known as Sir Vaseline Greece and his party-pieces were lengthy recitations, mostly by his favourite Oscar Wilde, and sometimes Shakespeare's *Julius Caesar* or James Joyce. Once at Saintbury he was delivering, "Friends, Romans, countrymen, lend me your ears." He flung his arm back and knocked poor old Mrs Parnell off the settee and on to the floor. Mother gave first aid with brandy. Sir Val's home was always lit by candlelight, Mother said so one could not see the dust. People would sing, recite, play the piano. I always thought my piano accordion was not quite *comme il faut*, but Sir Val and everyone loved it. It was of course always evening dress and it was a lovely evening that brought so many talented people together.

Apart from the house parties in the forties, the Gresham Hotel Saturday night dinner dances were all the go. There were showbands, songs like "September in the Rain" and "Deep Purple" and dances like the Lambeth Walk, rhumbas and foxtrots. The done thing was to order a table for eight or twelve and sometimes a rich Daddy—not mine—paid for everything. Otherwise, we each paid our own and shared a taxi home. I had such beautiful evening dresses, mostly made for me at Brown Thomas of Grafton Street.

At home, dinner parties were very formal, especially when my father's friends Colonel and Mrs Jourdaine came to stay for Horse Show week in August. They lived in Devonshire and the colonel had been my father's commanding officer in the Connaught Rangers during the action at Soupire when Father was hit, so it was an old friendship. They drank the King's health at dinner and talked army talk. The Jourdaines insisted on a dressing bell being rung at 6.30 pm. They would enter the drawing room for pre-dinner drinks, he in formal black tie and his dreary lady in a long lace gown.

My father never changed for dinner. "Damned old snob," he'd say, but just the same he, and indeed my Mother too, drunk or sober, always observed the proprieties. For example we would not dream of wearing bedroom slippers to dinner, even if it were only family. The wine was chilled or warmed, and always passed by father (at the head of the long table) to the right, port always to the left. I never saw paper serviettes. We had beautifully folded napkins shaped like a bishop's mitre or a water lily. The table looked a dream with beautiful silver and cut glass and the servants properly dressed and trained to wait table. The Parish Priest, Canon Sherwin, an awful long-winded bore, sat on my father's right. When we came to dessert and coffee the Canon would tell his ghost story. It took half an hour to tell and he himself looked ascetic and pale. Finally he presented the photograph of his ghost, which was passed round the table. It was a dim shape of a faceless man, in sixteenth century clothes! We never doubted Canon Sherwin because he was a gentle and saintly man. The odd part of it all was that however drunk Mother got, everyone pretended not to notice, as in the story of the Emperor's new clothes. She could belch, be funny or even bloody insulting and yet no one batted an eyelid. This was why I found my father hard to understand. He knew she would insult and belittle him, yet the dinner parties went on and on and in the earlier days the pregnancies every five years. It was all like some crazy game of let's pretend that everything is all right in the home of Major and Mrs O'Sullivan, when in truth everything was all wrong.

The house was very cold. Even in winter, only one fire was kept going in what we called the smoking room, because my Father smoked (twenty a day) and had his books and wireless set there. I had to entertain my friends in the huge freezing drawing room, with only a one-bar electric heater. I was always tense and nervous and afraid of Mother coming in. I gave them a glass of sherry and showed them masses of photographs of my film star sister. Mother went through a stage of being terribly dirty in every way, and God forgive me, I often dodged her, both on the roads and on the buses where she was particularly vociferous. But there was a happier side to life. Why is it, on looking back, that summers seem to have been so long and hot? We, Pat, Betty and myself spent a lot of time on Killiney beach. Life was very hospitable and those were the days of talking and laughing into the early hours.

Sherry parties from 4-6 pm were very much in but we never gave sherry parties, because we hated them. The noise and inebriated chatter did not appeal to my mother. Indeed she always found other people's parties lacking. Ours were the best, and I believe it was because of the mixture of ages. People from eighteen to eighty came and no one entering Saintbury was considered old. It was a Tír na n-Óg, almost a state of mind that denied age.

Maureen played the errant daughter in *The Barretts of Wimpole Street*, with Charles Laughton and Moira Shearer, and I played that part in real life. Father disapproved of all my boy friends. If I showed an interest in any particular fellow, he would say to Mother, "I hope Sheila isn't going to make a damned fool of herself." I wondered if he wanted me to be an old maid or if he simply did not like me because I was grown up. We never talked so I didn't know what he wanted me to be, or to do, and so I just drifted, always indecisive and lost. I had a variety of boyfriends from all walks of life, I didn't fall in love with any of them. The time had not come.

My next move was to join the Abbey Theatre School of acting. I had no Irish but got in because Shelagh Richards liked my audition. Frank Dermody was our teacher. In the class were Eithne Dunne, Maureen Kiely (later Cyril Cusack's wife) Kathleen Ryan and Wilfrid Brambell of the BBC's *Steptoe and*

Son fame. This was the forties, but Brambell, a Dubliner, looked old then and was a very quiet man.

We were all scared of Dermody, although he was a brilliant teacher. Lennox Robinson sometimes took classes, his trousers tied up with string. He was the most bumless man I have ever seen; from behind he looked like an empty suit. The training was first-class and helped me catch up on all that my West-Brit education had deprived me of—my own Irish culture.

One class that we all had a love-hate relationship with was Dermody's shooting class, which was also incredibly funny. One day he was trying to teach us how to fall flat on the floor. He could do it at the bang of a little theatre pistol because he could relax; that was the secret. We had a mattress to fall on. When Dermody fired we had to fall forward, throw our arms up and scream. The scream was easy. He got in such a frenzy about it all and used make such awful faces. We were terrified of damaging our bosoms, and also that one day he might put real bullets in the gun. I soldiered on for a year and graduated to the Peacock Theatre. I was a bit tired of the traditional Irish theatre and longed to dump *Juno and the Paycock* for a part in an Edgar Wallace drama. The really off-putting side to all this was that five nights a week I had to take the last train home to Killiney. It got in at 11.35 pm and I had a long walk home in the dark with no lights on the steep avenue leading up the hill to Saintbury. I was terrified because there was alleged to be a haunted crossroads where a phantom coach would cross one's path. At the top of the hill, Saintbury loomed dark and forbidding. I would let myself in, put on the bolt and chain and go to my room.

How can I write about what I believe was the

supernatural without being called a liar or neurotic? I lived with it for twenty-six years and heard it night after night: heavy footsteps hurrying, always hurrying, up the length of the corridor and stopping at the diningroom door. My bedroom was next to it. I dreaded hearing them and used pray I would be asleep before they came. On one of her visits home Maureen heard them and she moved into a hotel the next day. For a while, I even got used to it, but who was that earth-bound spirit who came every night on the same fruitless errand? I was very frightened of the supernatural, largely because my mother told me of ghosts when I was a child and often woke me in the night to tell me what apparition she had seen. We had adjoining rooms and I usually kept the door locked.

While I liked the Abbey School of Acting, I was still Hollywood starstruck. I wanted immediate fame without the hard climb up the ladder. I had never given much thought to marriage and what seemed to me then like the stagnation of settling down.

I had a couple of serious boy friends, one a pilot in the Royal Australian Air Force. He was a fine man but very anti-Roman Catholic. The next one, a naval type, was the same. I always ran into Protestants who didn't like the Catholic Church. Then, in the forties, the Church was very stringent. I always felt if I did meet someone I fancied that I had already queered my pitch. Fellows usually expected to be invited in to meet Father and Mother but I hadn't the guts to tell them about the situation at home: that my mother would probably be drunk and that she and my father only spoke to argue.

In the meantime a film director friend of my brother-in-law, John Farrow, called to visit us at Saintbury. Mother pounced on him immediately and asked him to give me a film test. His name was Eddie Goodman; he was fat, flash and fifty. He took me out to dinner to discuss business but he was a dirty old man, and it was a repeat of what happened in Hollywood. He wanted to know my vital statistics, and added that he would personally have to check them to be sure. While this conversation was going on Mr Eddie Goodman and I were sitting on a bench, at twilight, in the gardens of the Royal Marine Hotel, Dun Laoghaire. He was moving nearer and he said "Lift up your skirt and I'll check your legs." I called him a dirty old man and added "You may leave me home and consider yourself lucky if I don't tell Maureen and John Farrow." He was really non-plussed.

I discussed this with Mother and she said, "Let the old devil give you the film test." Once more the awful dieting. In the forties one had to be 10lbs under one's normal weight for the camera, which they said made you look bigger.

I left for London and stayed with my nice Aunt Maud in Hampstead. She promised to come with me every time I visited Denham Film Studios. Mr Goodman was consequently grumpy and ungracious. The day arrived for the test and I was three hours in make-up. Ever since, I've wondered what was wrong with my little face that they took so long working on it. Needless to add I did not pass that test. I was very naive to have believed I had even a chance.

I didn't mind too much, because I was having quite a social whirl in London, wining and dining at the Dorchester and Savoy, mostly with army friends of my brother Jack, who was then stationed at Aldershot. I had a woman theatrical agent who really believed in me and she arranged various auditions for me, but like a fool I went to a second agent whom a friend had recommended. Of course what happened was that neither of them wanted me then. Once again back to Ireland, home to Saintbury.

I was totally convinced that I was a failure. The spotlight was on my sister Maureen. She and her husband, John Farrow, were very much in with the hierarchy, as Maureen continued to have baby after baby, seven in all. She had started with three boys, Michael, Patrick and Johnnie, so she went to Lourdes to pray for a little girl. Her prayers were answered and she had a baby girl baptised by the Bishop of Lourdes, Maria de Lourdes, now Mia Farrow. Mia was followed by Prudence, Stephanie and Teresa. John had his papal title and they were looked on as a shining example in Sin City. As a result many visiting priests from America came to call on my father and mother.

On one occasion we had a visit from a Father John Murphy and his secretary Carl. He was full of news about the Farrows and very interesting about life in Hollywood. My parents took a fancy to him and his friend and invited them to stay for a couple of days. I do remember thinking that Father Murphy had very dirty fingernails for a priest. They stayed from Friday to Monday and then left with messages for Maureen and promises to write. On Tuesday my Mother found we had been robbed. It was a cleanout—all the good heavy linen, silver, cutlery, jewellery and several valuable ornaments. The "priest" was a well known conman and thief, as was his friend Carl, who was wanted for murder in the United States. They had departed at dawn and the infuriating part of it all was that the previous night the priest had asked us all to kneel down for his blessing. What a laugh he must have had!

My mother, though, as ever, drinking heavily, was generous to a fault. She was a snob and then paradoxically could become an out and out socialist. For example she "made free," as my Father put it, by gossiping with the servants, and going down to the village and gossiping with the villagers. She would dispense glossy pictures of Maureen among them, and bask in what she imagined was the reflected glory. Just as suddenly she would become haughty and say she hated the lower classes. In those days that fraternisation was not on. Even in church, the congregation was divided and the upper classes or moneyed people went up front and put a shilling in the plate at the church door. A brass rail divided us from the poor who sat at the back and put a penny in the plate.

We got our clothes from Brown Thomas in Grafton Street. They went on Mother's account which Father paid. We went out for the day when the account came in because there was always one hell of a row. My father was very hard to get money out of and Mother used make up lists and leave these lists on his desk. The lists would be "Chemist, STs for the three girls, Odorono, toothpaste." There was always hell over what he called "that damned Odonoro. Why can't they use soap like everyone else," he'd bark! But if there was a list, he'd always leave the money, which was divided between us for fags and lipsticks. He maintained he was teaching us the value of money. Poor Betty, the youngest, came off the worst, because while Pat and I would fight to get our clothes at Brown Thomas she was left with our cast-offs. It didn't matter because she was so pretty.

One other crude aspect of our family life was that

every Thursday afternoon my mother slipped into my father's bedroom and locked the door. The blind was pulled down and there wasn't a sound. For quite a number of years I wondered about this but as I got older the penny dropped. I used to watch Mother, from the top of the stairs, coming out of his room with two half-crowns, five shillings for sex and I often thought, I'm only a result of five bob's worth, and I was born steeped in John Jameson, some start for a life.

I was leading a waster's life and consequently was depressed. A priest I detested, Father O'Sullivan, preached a sermon about "the idle daughters of the well-to-do," how he would meet them loitering. He suggested the technical schools and all this with his eyes fixed on me in the front pew! I told Father and he said, "I don't need those damned fellows to tell me how to bring up a family." He *did* have his very good points and loyalty was one.

19 Marriage and Estrangement

One wet and windy night, I was invited on a blind date to a party in the neighbouring village of Dalkey. It was a black night but with the optimism of youth I was not concerned. When I arrived there was a crowd of young people in the small house. The fellow I might have fancied seemed to be fixed up with a girl friend. Little did I know that the quiet fellow whom I had absolutely no interest in at all, Jimmy Mooney, was to be my husband. I had not thought about marriage, I vaguely imagined that one day I would be ensconced in a large house with servants, a nanny for my children, and the man of my choice was a shadowy figure.

That night Jimmy Mooney saw me home. He had a big old-fashioned bicycle. I learned that he was a dental surgeon in practice with his father and that they were both famous yachtsmen. I liked living beside the sea, I always have, I loved swimming in it, but I detested being on it. Not only was I a very bad sailor but I was very frightened of it. My years of toing and fro-ing on the old mail boats to various boarding schools in England, had quite finished me off where the sea was concerned. Jimmy asked me out quite a bit, always to the yacht club.

At home the parties were still full swing. We planned a fancy dress ball. This particular party was a welcome home for my brother Jackie. He had been in the war, transferred from his regiment The King's Own Royal Regiment to the Paratroopers. He was in the drop at Arnhem and was taken prisoner of war in Germany for the latter part of the war. I took in the telegram from the war office, which read: "We regret to inform that Major John Charles O'Sullivan is posted missing believed killed." I remember after the initial shock the utter relief because I *knew* Jackie was alive. So did Mother who said, "I *feel* he's alive and well." Everyone was amazed because Mother and I went to a big ball in Shangannagh Castle Hotel after we got the news. But poor Father was in a terrible state. He kept saying "damn my daughters, I want my son." However it ended happily. My brother kept a diary when he was a prisoner which only Father was allowed to read. He said it was horrific, especially being kept in solitary confinement in the dark for six months. Jackie confessed that he kept his sanity by saying his Rosary over and over.

My mother wrote half the invitations for the fancy dress and ball and I wrote the other half. This was a fatal arrangement, because she put the wrong day on hers. I'll never forget one evening seeing an aged Punch and Judy, cap and bells, strolling down the drive, followed by a vintage Rolls Royce weighed down by a massive Falstaff, Sir Valentine Grace. Mother told Essie the parlour-maid to say that no one was in: "Tell them they've come on the wrong day."

All the following weeks up to June 12th, D-day, visions were appearing coming blithely down the drive and the nervous strain was awful.

The day before the ball, following procedure, I pawned my diamond bracelet to pay for the band. Father locked his piano, and the usual tinny hired piano arrived. Father was duly booked into a hotel for the night. The fancy dress ball was unforgettable. The night was warm with the scent of flowers and even the moon shone obligingly, over Killiney Bay. Young, middle aged and very old all came and indulged their particular fantasies by dressing up in whatever they had always secretly imagined themselves to be. We always mixed the ages at our parties, which was lovely and added to the success of those wonderful nights.

I watched the parade in the lovely room overlooking the bay: Scarlett O'Hara, fairies, gnomes, Nero, a bunch of medical students dressed up as fullbusted nurses. Whenever I'm sad I recall that parade in my home, I turn it on like a video and recall the past. There were a hundred people waiting to welcome my brother home. He refused to come out of his bedroom and stayed there with the door locked for the entire party. He did let about six chosen friends in, including a girl friend of mine whom he had taken a fancy to, and indeed was later to marry. She was an attractive Killiney girl, Marie Roche. We had to pretend that one of the guests was the brother. We chose a tall man dressed as an Arab, his face covered with a yashmak. He graciously received all the adulation and congratulations!

Jimmy Mooney and I went out together quite a lot. The courtship was long and drawn-out with a lot of heated arguments over religion, Jimmy having been brought up a strict Protestant. Then we were both invited to a wedding in Belfast. I think the fact that I flirted with a charmer from the North brought things to a head. Finally Jimmy and I got engaged. In a typically Irish way he proposed. He had left me home one night and had about three minutes to catch the last bus. As he ran off he shouted, "Ask your father about it."

"About what?" I said.

"Getting married," said he. Sadly my engagement was just about the unhappiest time of my life. In the 1940s mixed marriages were very difficult indeed, and in my case the word difficult was a vast understatement. Jimmy insisted that he would never sign his future children over to Rome. This would mean that I could not marry in a Catholic Church, and if I married outside it I would be excommunicated. I was sad too. In those days every girl had a dream of a nice wedding. I didn't have the guts to tell my father. My mother told him and to put it very mildly he was not keen at all. He, religion apart, did not like the Mooney family. He called them "rough diamonds" and "pot hunters" because Jimmy and his father won virtually all the yachting prizes.

We bought the ring. It was very small. The one I wanted was bigger, but I choose the smallest out of decency and it turned out to be the most expensive. When I showed Father the ring, he said, "very nice," and added, "I hope Mooney understands he has to toe the line as far as the children are concerned." I felt awful because I knew Jimmy would not give in. I just nodded, "Yes, Father."

In the forties, we really were dominated by the Church and the clergy. They were, to my mind, totally autocratic and male-chauvinist. Our curate, Father

O'Sullivan caused me to be more unhappy than ever. He had never liked me and regarded me with suspicion because I had lots of boy friends! Little did he know that, like a large number of young people of my era, I was strictly moral as regards sex. The most we ever did was a bit of a court, which usually provoked guilt and was spoiled by recounting it in confession. I made my mind up, or at least we did, that as Jimmy was adamant and would not sign the form that any children would be Roman Catholic, we would marry in the Protestant Church and the children would be Protestants if they were boys and Catholics if they were girls. Of course this did not satisfy my own Church. I was not happy as it was the religion I had been brought up in and though I outwardly denied it, to use an old idiom, "I had the faith." I refused to give in on the basis that if I said no to Jimmy's requests he would leave me! Things were, as ever, bad at home. I wanted out, a marriage and children and a chance to be happy.

Once again I was afraid, so Mother went to tell Father. He said, "If Sheila goes against my wishes she'll get no quarter from me." He would disinherit me and never again have anything to do with me. I had the choice. That dreaded day came when Mother announced that my father would see Jimmy and me in his study. The dialogue went thus: my father said, "Can you support Sheila in the manner to which she is accustomed?"

Jimmy lied bravely, "I can."

Then my Father said "Sheila knows if she marries outside the Church I'm finished with her. Even Canon Barker (the Protestant Rector next door) would agree."

Then Jimmy said, "Can she stay here until we get

154

married?"

"Oh yes, I want no unpleasantness like that, but when she leaves I'm finished with her."

A few wedding presents started to arrive. I laid them out sadly in a spare bedroom. Then there was this awful façade, the celebration dinner party. A few old friends and the Mooney family, Jimmy's father and step-mother to be, Mildred, were put at the end of the long table as far away from my father as possible. He was at his coldest; the only conversation he had with the Mooneys was a few desultory remarks about the weather. Mother, astonishingly, rose to the occasion and stayed sober. She always took my part. It was one hell of an evening. Jimmy and I went to see the Rector of Monkstown parish church, a very nice ex-RAF man. He must have given the situation some thought. He didn't say much and certainly did not try to convert me. All he did say was, "If you have any trouble afterwards come and see me." We arranged a wedding date of January 20th. Mother would give me away. I had no real trousseau, just a new hat, and for the last time I charged a new suit on Brown Thomas's account. I'm sorry now I didn't run up one hell of a bill.

I had five shillings in my bag when I got married! The day arrived and I was packed and ready to leave. That morning I went down to say goodbye to Father. Mother was listening on the top of the stairs. It was nine o'clock and he was in bed reading his *Irish Times*, pince-nez glasses on the end of his nose. I said to him, "I'm off now, Father." I didn't dare kiss him or go near him.

He looked at me over his glasses with those pale blue eyes and said, "Well, I hope you'll be happy, but I don't think you will." Then he added, "There's an envelope on the mantelpiece. Take it and don't answer it." I took the envelope and my eyes filled up, I said, "Goodbye then," but he'd gone back to his *Irish Times*. I saw that it was upside down.

When we got to Monkstown the hackney driver, who had known us for years, drove straight to the Catholic Church. He looked astonished when Mother said, "No, the Protestant one."

I had a moment of panic, "I'm not getting married. Mother replied, "Quite right, we'll go home."

"How could you?" I retorted and marched into the church. It was a nice little ceremony: Jimmy's father and step-mother, a few close friends and Mother to give me away.

After a luncheon in a Dublin hotel, given by my father-in-law, we left for our London honeymoon. I opened Father's letter; there was a cheque for £100. "He's coming round!" we both said. He was not! We went everywhere in London, the Savoy, the Dorchester and to plenty of good shows. Then back to start a new life in suburbia, but happily still near the sea, further up the coast from Killiney to Sandycove. Our home was a three-up three-down little house. In the beginning I could not like it, I despised it, my heart was always in Saintbury. I couldn't cook; I had no idea at all; I'd never had to. I had never done any housework and found it boring and exhausting. We bought all cheap furniture, awful stuff, with the idea that one day we would replace it but we never did.

I got pregnant and my doctor told me my baby was due the end of November. We were both delighted and no one was more pleased than my mother. It was a harmonious nine months. Then one night I woke up with a terrible pain in my lower back. The pain was acute, like a rat gnawing into my back. I got out of our bed and went and lay in a tumble of blankets on a bed in the spare room. I didn't want to disturb Jimmy because his first patient was at eight forty-five. Next day was worse. I had violent attacks of shivering when I became frozen, and then roasting, my night-dress soaked in perspiration. These were rigours. I was very ill. My gynaecologist came out to see me and I was immediately moved to hospital. I was put on four-hourly penicillin and a foul tasting compound, fittingly named potszit. I had an acute kidney infection, pyelitis. The danger was that my unborn baby was feeling the same terrible heat and cold that I was. I had several more trips to hospital to be treated for this painful condition. When my child was due to be born, I was ill again, so I was not allowed any sedation, in case my already weakened baby might die. After an agonising labour and forceps and stitches, I gave birth to my little six pounds girl, Pauline Anne.

When I saw my baby for the first time, I decided that childbirth is the only worthwhile form of torture. Three days later, I felt something inside me snap—I was having a haemorrhage. Anyone who has had one will know how frightening this is. Blood just pumps and pumps. Bells rang, a doctor and emergency team appeared. "Get her gynaecologist," someone said. I felt very weak, I was terrified to see a priest sitting beside me. He told me that I was in "some danger" and because of that, even though I had been excommunicated, he could give me the last sacraments. This near death experience has been told many times, but I do not care. I am happy to be able to relate my own and ever since I have had no fear whatever of death. I felt I was floating and I could hear voices calling me. I knew I was leaving the room and going away somewhere. There was peace and a warm light and with total detachment I could see myself below in the bed. The light was drawing me into a vortex, a tunnel. At the end of it were people, all chanting "come, come" and then a voice said, "your hour has not yet come." I heard my baby cry; it was over. I was frustrated for two hours before I got over it. I had not wanted to come back. That experience left me convinced that after death there is another form of life.

So it was back to suburbia and our little house. Mother devised a plan to try and win over my father. She took Pauline, my three week old baby, to see him. I well remember the day. It was summer and he was sitting, in his usual spot, under the fig tree. It was such a beautiful-looking tree and it bore fruit. Every year a very aristocratic old lady, a Miss Netterfield, would come with her basket to collect the figs. She was known as "Figgy face." From an upstairs window I watched my mother cross the lawn with my baby. I heard my father bark, "Take that damned child away." Mother said, "It's not the baby's fault," and put his grandchild in his arms. My eyes were full of tears.

That night when I undressed Pauline I found a pound note tucked in her matinee coat. Written on it were the words, "Buy her a doll." Life can be very sad. My father was never going to relent.

The end of an era was approaching, Saintbury was a very big house and it was becoming impossible to get domestic help. The house was dusty, neglected and lonely, with my father at his club every day and Mother out drinking.

One slattern after another came and went, and with them went various things they pinched. The garden too was running down and a couple of the greenhouses were left to decay.

20 Father's Death

Father was a lonely introverted man. Not only that, he was delicate and had suffered five bouts of pneumonia. There was no penicillin then, so he had to fight his way through crises, the border line between life and death. When my baby, Pauline, was a year old, Father became seriously ill. It was pneumonia again and he was moved into the Merrion Nursing Home in Dublin. Maureen came home from America. He was dying. I was terribly upset. It was no use my going to see him, because he had already declared that he did not want to see me or Mother. "She's been a bad and useless wife to me," he told Maureen, who took a room next to his to be near him all the time. The home was run by a Miss Barrett, a war veteran, a proper old warrior. She wore her medal ribbons, and her patients included many who had served with HM Forces. Father thought a lot of her and she was a great nurse.

The family kept a vigil so that Father was never alone. Finally I went to see him, taking care to go when he was unconscious. I held his hand and he opened his eyes, those very blue eyes, and stared at me. As soon as he realised who it was, he hissed and hissed—he was too weak to speak. It was one of the most horrifying incidents of my life and there are no words that can express my feelings. I ran out of the room,

I thought what a strange woman my mother was. Prior to my Father's last illness, I found her up to her elbows in soap suds and blue/red water. "What are you doing?" I asked and she replied, "I saw the man in black pass the window, so I'm washing the Union Jack. Your Father wants to be wrapped in it when he dies." This was the flag that always adorned the regimental picture "Recruiting of the Connaught Rangers."

Father died two months after that episode. The flag was clean and ready and at his own express wishes his remains were wrapped in the Union Jack. He died on Christmas Eve 1972, while the morning Angelus was ringing. Heavy snowflakes were falling and tapping the window pane with gentle fingers. Inside the room, his wife, his son, his three daughters. I was the fourth daughter but I had been cast out a long time before. Maureen, always his favourite, had flown in from New York just in time. She held a lighted candle in his hand, the candle that is symbolic of life. His poor crippled hand, that result of the Battle of the Somme that he had always been so conscious of, was tucked under the bedclothes. I, of course, stood away at the end of the bed, the prodigal who was never forgiven.

I watched my Father die, knowing that he had not forgiven me, that I had this to remember for the rest of my life. The Angelus stopped ringing, a nurse blew out the candle, he had breathed his last. *Vita mutator non tollitur*. The last of the Victorian O'Sullivans, the end of an era. I had never known him. I could not be what he wanted me to be. I went home alone, branded by my family as a drop-out and a liar. I was not either of those things. I crossed roads and did not look right or left; I hoped a car would knock me down. Winter sunshine suddenly filtered through the leaden skies; tears had frozen on my face. The gates of Heaven are open for the twelve days of Christmas in honour of the twelve Apostles. Pious platitudes for the dead but what about the living, forced to walk about with a knife in their gut? Nietzsche wrote, "Thus spoke the Devil to me once. Even God has His hell, It is His love for man."

The family took my father's remains to Cork to be interred in the O'Sullivan vault in the Victorian cemetery, Saint Joseph's. We stayed the night in the Imperial Hotel. I shared a room with my sisters Pat and Betty. It was very cold and we spread our black funeral coats over our feet. I looked at the three coats; there was something very sad about them. Mother shared an adjoining room with Maureen, who said she had a bad night. In her sleep, Mother kept singing, "Abide with me." Like the proverbial Chinaman she showed neither joy nor grief. She said she had been "fond of him (Father) in her own way."

The O'Sullivan aunts and cousins, strict Roman Catholics, were icy cold to me. I was a disgrace, excommunicated from the Church. When I held out my hands, Aunt Florence, Father's eldest sister, gave me a limp handshake and stared over my head, pale cold blue eyes like my Father's. There was a Christmas fancy-dress dance in the hotel, and there we were all in black, like a flock of crows. Not so, Maureen; she scintillated and she and Mother out-did each other for wit and repartee at the dinner table.

This was my first contact with death and I was

deeply shocked at the terrible morbidity and my own unbelievable grief. The vault was like a large room and Mother insisted on going in to have a look: "I've always taken care of my husband's accommodation," she said to a priest who did not think it advisable "because of the fumes." The name-plates gleamed on the old oak coffins; an aperture let in light. Going back to 1881 they looked perfect. Mother later remarked, "The devil went in there to polish the brasses." Over the portico of the vault were the words "And God shall wipe away all tears, and death shall be no more." They closed the doors of the vault and that part of my life was over.

I returned home to Jimmy and baby Pauline, but there was to be more humiliation for me. I bought the Sunday papers as usual after Mass. To my horror the headlines across the front page were "Major O'Sullivan's £86,000"—a lot of money in those days. They had listed the amounts bequeathed to each member of the family. At the bottom of the list for everyone to read: "To my daughter Sheila I leave the sum of one hundred pounds free of legacy duty."

I bore my Father no malice then, nor do I now. He was a Victorian, a man of his time, and that is the way he thought and acted. And, as he said, "you have the choice between that man or me."

21

Back
in
the
Fold

Soon I became pregnant again. In due course I gave
birth to a son, William. There was a cloud on the
horizon when Jimmy said, "This one is to be
Protestant." I am not a bigot, but it is a fact that
everyone wants their child to have the same religion
they were brought up to believe in.

I had given birth to this child and I thought, "damn
the Mooney family to hell!" I felt a fierce resentment.
But time, too much time, went by, and when I could
barely squeeze my large masculine baby into the
ridiculous flippancies of a christening gown, left open
down the back because of his girth, he was christened
by Arthur Butler (now Archbishop of Tuam), the
charming man who had married us.

I was not happy and being excommunicated from
my church made me quite determined I would get
back. It is a lonely feeling being on the outside looking
in. In time, my son, William, and his sister Pauline
were attending a nursery school in nearby Dalkey. A
dear old lady, Miss Moore, was their teacher. She

knew my son was to be brought up a Protestant but I had the feeling she was feeding him large doses of Catholicism. A curate in my parish, Glasthule, started taking an interest in my case, that in the eyes of the Catholic Church I was living in the state of mortal sin, and my children were bastards. I cannot think of a crueller concept.

Then the time came for Pauline to be confirmed, aged twelve. She missed out at the convent through illness, so it was arranged for her to go with the local children to our parish church. I dressed her in a long frock. It was the only one in the church, and with her long fair hair she looked lovely. Father Bergin, who had business on his mind, took her by the hand up the long aisle to the Archbishop John Charles McQuaid. The Archbishop confirmed her, and, turning to Father Bergin, said, "The time has come to be kind to her mother."

Meanwhile, Jimmy was going to the Olympics in Helsinki, to represent Ireland in the dragon class in yachting. Whether he felt guilty for always leaving me behind, or whether he did not feel competent to pass on his religion to his son, I shall never know, but as he left the house he turned round and said, "you can have William. Take him to Mass on Sunday." So I had to tell Father Bergin that though Jimmy had agreed to his son, then seven, being brought up a Catholic, he would not sign any papers to agree to his children being Roman Catholic. They got around that one by stating that if I would promise to go on living with this man (for better or worse!) and promise to do my best with the children, they would honour the promises as a recognition of my marriage, and my children as legitimate.

Next I had to go to confession. My first for thirteen

years! I could have gone to confession any day, any time. But no, the confession was arranged for ten-twenty on a Sunday. Mass was due to start at ten-thirty and the Church was packed. Father Bergin had told me to sit outside his box, half way down the aisle. At ten-twenty sharp, out of the sacristy appeared His Reverence and into his box. I went in, every head turned and as I came out another woman went to go in. Father Bergin waved her away. "That was a private confession," he said. I don't know what I felt, probably a bit angry because Jimmy and I were good and legally married in the eyes of the law. My penance was a decade of the Rosary and I went up to communion on the wings of a dove. I was happy to be back in the fold whatever the cost.

22 Mother's Death

Dark clouds were beginning to gather. We kept budgies and the blue one got out and flew away. I watched in despair as the tiny bird flew up into the dark sky; there was a thunderstorm coming. Mother always said, "If the blue bird flies away happiness goes out the window."

At this time, my Mother was living in a lovely flat overlooking the sea in Monkstown, quite near us, on the same stretch of coast. My sisters, Pat and Betty, lived with her. Mother had been very restless, moving from house to house; she was getting old and it was too much for her. My youngest sister, Betty, was with her when she got a stroke. Suddenly she could not speak and got a weakness all down the right side of her body. My heart went out to my mother and the extraordinary thing was that she could still laugh, laugh at the queer sounds she made when she tried to speak. I never saw her cry. I asked her once, "Didn't you ever cry?" and she said, "No, I have never cried."

"But why?" I said.

Of course I got one of her typical answers: "crying ruins one's eyes." I often think that I did all her crying for her, though I love Spinoza's admonition, "neither weep nor laugh but understand."

Mother was moved to the Merrion Nursing Home where Father had died and put under the kindly but militant eye of Matron, Miss Barrett. After a while her speech returned, but mentally she was in a bad way and becoming too troublesome for the orderly nursing home. She was seeing doves flying by the window and, worse, she saw a leprechaun. I nearly began to see it myself. She was sent back to her flat but things grew worse. She declared she kept seeing the "man in black," the devil. Then there would be a terrible fracas: Mother would shout and yell and beat the devil with her umbrella. Usually this took place in her bedroom. She went really berserk and we were all terrified. Once her devil was slain, she would sing "Onward Christian soldiers" and then call out, "You can come in, it's all over." Two nurses were engaged but they were not much use. One used throw holy water into the room and it made Mother worse. Strangely, she said to me, in one of her lucid moments, "You can come in when the fight's on, I would never hurt you." I knew that to be true, because I knew that in her strange way she loved me.

When Mother seemed more composed we thought it safe to ask a few people in for drinks, and everything was going very well and we were all relaxed and happy. I noticed as the night wore on, that one of our guests, a middle-aged blonde with a shrill voice, was monopolising the conversation and Mother seemed left out. She never liked to be left out. Next I heard through the babble of voices a low humming noise, I said sotto voice to my sister Pat, "Do you hear what I hear?" She listened and nodded. I said, "I hope to God she's not going to fly." She was; the revving noise was getting louder and louder. The blonde woman looked on in terror. Then with arms akimbo my poor Mother was airborne! A nice polite man put his hand over hers and said, "There, there, you're tired." She was impervious and everyone else was paralysed. I knew the worst was to come—the crash landing. It came with heavy drama and awful noise.

Everyone was shattered. We were totally embarrassed. Mother said, "I hate flying. Would anyone like another drink?" She made no reference to the hiatus; it was all as if it had never happened.

Things grew progressively worse. Doctors were unanimous: Mother would have to be "put away." It was a terrible hospital, obviously for very disturbed cases. The drive in the taxi, a long drive, was awful. My heart was in my boots but Mother was oblivious to the whole thing. A big fat Matron with a large bunch of keys jangling on her belt received us. We went through doors and she unlocked and then locked every single one.

Mother's room overlooked the garden. It was nice and bright but there was no handle inside the door and unbreakable glass in the window, which only opened two inches. Just as we were going in, two nurses with a tea trolley appeared and unlocked the door next to hers. One of them said "Stand back there, stand back," there was a hell of a crash and the food was thrown into the corridor. My God, I thought, I am leaving my mother in a lunatic asylum. The word asylum kept drumming into my head.

I looked out of the window. In the garden the patients were wandering around. One old lady was dancing a quiet minuet, an idiot man was laughing heartily at whatever went on in his head. There was a Jesus, arms raised, preaching gently. It was like a twilight zone, an awful place betwixt life and death.

I used of course go and visit Mother. She kept on and on about this leprechaun and would ask me countless times to put him out the window. She told me how he upset her face-powder on the dressing table and was always climbing on the pelmet where he would sit making faces at her. Meanwhile at home, life went on in a mundane way. There is nothing poetic about housework. My children Pauline and William were my only joy. Suburbia was eating into my soul, diminishing me. How I missed Saintbury.

Mother eventually came home almost cured. Father had left her a tiny annuity and she had not the money to drink. I did not know then that most of the time she was actually hungry as she was supporting her sister, my Aunt Mona, who feigned a bad heart and was as strong as a bull!

After six years I was pregnant again. I was delighted; Jimmy was not! "Why don't you go to the North and buy some penny royal?" he said. I had a lovely baby girl, Wendy. All those years ago in the convent at Kensington, I had looked down from my window at Peter Pan in Kensington Gardens. Jimmy made me call my son William, after his father, but at least I had my Wendy.

My husband's world was sailing. He had three bronze medals for Ireland and was the only Irishman to bring the Duke of Edinburgh Cup (for Dragons) home to Ireland. I felt very left out. I was snobbish about our little home full of cheap furniture. Immature, but I excuse myself because I grew up in a big house in the days of gracious living.

Mother came to lunch with me on her usual

Thursday. She'd had her hair retinted bright blonde. Two things worried me. She would never take her coat off, but that day she spilled soup on it, so she took it off to mop it up. I was absolutely horrified to see that she was emaciated. The second thing was that she said she'd a queer pressure pain at the base of her neck and added, "I think I'm in for the knock." I dismissed that, because she was always saying it. But she seemed far away, I felt uneasy.

At about three in the morning I had a nightmare. I thought I was choking and I couldn't breath. I shouted and woke Jimmy, I had felt in the dream that I was Mother. I said, "I've got to phone her."

Jimmy was furious. "At this hour? Go back to sleep. I've got a patient at eight-thirty." After a lot of tossing and restlessness I slept until the alarm went off at seven-fifteen. With the usual rush of breakfast and packed lunches for school, I shoved my nightmare into the background. At ten o'clock the phone rang; it was Jimmy. "Yes?" I said, wondering if I had done something wrong.

"I'm afraid it's your Mother," he said. From far away I heard my own voice ask, "Is she dead?" I had known in the early hours of the morning when I'd had that nightmare. Later the doctor confirmed that she died at about three in the morning, the time I had woken up screaming that I wanted to phone her.

When I got to my mother's flat, Aunt Mona, who had brought in her morning tea and found her dead, was in a state of collapse. Mother had died of a massive stroke. I went into Mother's room where a nurse was starting to lay her out. "Would you leave us alone for a few minutes?" I said. My Mother had gone, but she would never leave me as long as I lived, she would always be in my heart. I knelt beside her and took her cold, so cold hand. I prayed, "Dear God for whatever she did forgive her, and let her know the peace she never had in life." For me it was different from any other death, it was the severing of a spiritual umbilical cord, the closest of all relationships, my biological mother. Maria Eva, my mother, looked lovely. In life she was always very vain. She was laid out in blue with pink rosebuds in her hands. I could see in her serene face something of the beautiful girl she had been.

Respecting her wishes I put her two Christian Science books in the coffin and a little statue of Holy Mary, whom she always disliked. This was a gesture to her sense of humour. I looked at her for the last time. One dies so many times inside one's self. My eyes were blinded with tears. I remembered the beautiful words of Tagore: "Death is not extinguishing the light but putting the lamp out because the dawn has come." They closed the coffin. With her passing, that part of my life, the agonising struggle to love my parents, the hope of a little love and some recognition, was over.

Nine years later my husband Jimmy died in agony with cancer. I suffered five years of depressive illness, hospitalisation, drugs and shock treatment. I have survived because I believe I have inherited some of my Father's fortitude and most of all because Mother left me her greatest legacy, her sense of humour.

Epilogue

I went back to Saintbury one day while it was empty. It was torture. I walked through the empty rooms. I seemed to hear voices, children laughing, a piano tinkling, even my dog barking far away. The huge empty drawing room, the golden embossed wallpaper was peeling in damp strips, sunlight picked up clouds of dust, phantoms dancing and the strains of a dance band.

I cried for a week after that visit. Now that lovely old house is cut down the middle and made into two houses. The red creeper doesn't grow up the walls any more. I don't blame it!

And damn to hell whoever cut down the willow trees.

Strange Vagabond of God
The Story of John Bradburne

Fr John Dove SJ

A re-issue of this popular and significant book

This is the story of the life of a remarkable religious service, in Europe, the Holy Land and Africa. Poet, mystic, hermit and vagabond, John Bradburne's strange life was devoted to the welfare of others and also a ceaseless quest for God. Since his death, there have been moves towards a campaign for his beatification.

POOLBEG

Women Surviving
Studies in the History of Irish Women in the 19th and 20th centuries

Edited by

Maria Luddy and Cliona Murphy

This highly original collection of historical articles addresses aspects of women's history in nineteenth and early twentieth-century Ireland, including: nuns in society; paupers and prostitutes; the impact of international feminists on the Irish suffrage movement and women's contribution to post-Independence Irish politics.

POOLBEG

The Poolbeg Golden Treasury of Well Loved Poems

Edited by Sean McMahon

By the compiler of *Rich and Rare*

and

The Poolbeg Book of Children's Verse

A delightful anthology of everyone's favourite poems, from Shakespeare to Patrick Kavanagh

POOLBEG

In Quiet Places
The Uncollected Stories, Letters and Critical Prose of Michael McLaverty

Edited with an Introduction by Sophia Hillam King

This collection provides a unique and fascinating insight into the mind and artistic development of one of Ireland's finest writers

POOLBEG